IF IT WAS EASY, JESUS

Our country has never been so ravaged by division, not in my life-time. Here's a critical call to unity. How timely! And Dave hits the issues (including racism) head on, but with sensitivity and grace. Chapter 1 gives us a great entree into the book, so you don't want to stop there. Dave tells us where he's going before he goes. He is fun to read and easy to follow, and the points he makes are relevant and needful! He is gifted and engaging as a writer with an upbeat style. He is not preaching at us. His own vulnerability makes us feel like we're together. I particularly appreciated Chapter 6. Stories stick, and he has some choice ones. The fact that they are doing what he's talking about in Tucson makes the book credible. His occasional Bible studies are lively and illuminating. Each chapter includes helpful questions. Dave, you did it again! Way to go.

—PAUL ANDERSON
Former Director of International Lutheran Renewal, Founder of Master's Institute and Alliance of Renewal Churches

David Drum has written what he's living. I've heard Dave say and practice many of the things in this book as we have partnered to see our city transformed. I've had the honor to follow in Dave's footsteps as he's helped lead the pastors of our city to greater racial unity. Our church has been in the center of addressing the needs in foster care and of orphans and Dave led the way in that effort. I can go almost chapter by chapter and identify how these principles and practices have been employed in and through our church and I thank God how he has used Dave to encourage us. My point is that this book is way more than theory. It is God's truth that has been applied to make a difference by bringing the influence of God to our city. This is one of those few 'must read' books.

—GLEN ELLIOTT
Lead Pastor, Pantano Christian Church, Tucson, AZ

David Drum has produced yet another excellent work on the unity of the body of Christ. Dave not only teaches and writes about this unity based on John 17, but he does the hard work of producing this unity in our city! His orthodoxy is his orthopraxy; he studies, prays, and works for the unity of the City Church. In this book, he outlines the secrets of the kingdom and also gives practical stories of how God in Tucson is unifying His body to bring city transformation, the fulfillment of Jesus' prayer, and glory to God. This is an important work for all cities desiring to see His kingdom come and His will being done!

—RANDY REYNOLDS
Executive Director, Community Renewal, Tucson, AZ

David Drum is a friend who has faithfully stewarded his role as a leader in Tucson's gospel movement. I appreciate how he draws us back to God's heart for unity and engagement. A spirit of humility and unity is crucial if faith leaders want to be effective in engaging their cities during such a divisive time in our history.

—KEVIN PALAU
Author of *Unlikely: Setting Aside our Differences to Live Out the Gospel,* and President and CEO, Luis Palau Association

For over 10 years our school district quietly met with church leaders on a regular basis and partnered with their churches on an annual event. Then 4Tucson came along and provided both encouragement and tangible support. The level of participation and joint projects in our district steadily increased. Other school districts also responded to the opportunity to partner and communicate with churches. The shift was most significant and would not have happened without David's vision and the humble service of 4Tucson staff.

—CALVIN BAKER
Superintendent, Vail Unified School District, Vail, AZ

The Willow Creek Association is committed to the singular idea that inspired, encouraged, and equipped Christian leaders transform their communities. The leaders we serve are not just full-time ministry staff, but leaders in all sectors of society committed to pursuing their grander visions—whatever they might be. Since 2013, it has been our privilege to partner with 4Tucson to leverage the Summit to help develop leaders in all domains of interest in Tucson. The stories of success are detailed in David Drum's latest book. I believe this book will be a source of inspiration as you consider how your leadership can join with others to create a grander vision for your city.

—WESLEY KING
Regional Director, Willow Creek Association, South Barrington, IL

En los años que Dios me ha permitido vivir en Tucson, he conocido personas que han impactado mi vida, por ser gente integra (que lo que piensan y hablan eso es lo que hacen), así es David Drum un hombre íntegro, que puedo oírlo hablar de la unidad, sus principios y resultados, porque él lo practica, en este libro encontraras historias y relatos verídicos que te ayudaran, a entender y a practicar la unidad que Jesús oro que tuviéramos.

In the years that God has allowed me to live in Tucson, I have met people who have impacted my life because they are integral people (what they think and speak is what they do). David Drum is a man of integrity because not only can I hear him talk about unity—its principles and results—but he also practices it. In this book, you will find stories and results that will help you understand and practice the unity that Jesus prayed we would have.

—ANGEL MORFIN
Lead Pastor, Peniel Church, Tucson, AZ

In this book, David Drum takes us back to the prayer of Jesus to discover unity in the Body of Christ. This is not a call for more wasted paper, time, and energy on ecumenical agreements; this is a call to recognize the sovereignty of God. The church belongs to Jesus, called out and bound together by the Spirit, and created by the Father. David helps the reader to see the radical nature of unity, the obstacles we place in its way, and the efforts of the evil one to destroy it. The solution is an invitation; even more, a challenge to pray through those things that divide the Body of Christ without sacrificing the unique gifts each "family of faith" brings to the table. This is the unity for which Jesus prayed, and continues to pray even to this day. There is no one more able to challenge the whole church than this "employee of John 17," Pr. David Drum. I commend this book to all who long for unity in the Body of Christ.

—MARK VANDERTUIG
Service Coordinator, Lutheran Congregations in Mission for Christ

From Dave's first book *Jesus Surprising Strategy* and now *If It Was Easy, Jesus Wouldn't Have Prayed For It*, it's plain to see that God continues to use David Drum to keep before the Church the importance of prayer and unity. Dave has captured the fact that unity is one of the essential elements necessary for the world to truly see us (or the church) as God's people. Any pastor and people who truly treasure the harvest, and see unity and prayer as a priority for their body as well as the greater Body of Christ, must read and apply the principles of this book.

—APOSTLE WARREN ANDERSON
Lead Pastor, Living Waters Ministries, Tucson, AZ

We live in a polarized, hostile world, but people like David Drum give us hope. This is a significant and timely book which addresses the critical issues we face in our homes, our churches, and our cities. Dave isn't just an idea man. He's a practitioner. He's been faithful to God's calling to make a difference in his city, Tucson, but the influence of his life and ministry touch our state and nation. It's a new day, a day the Lord has made, for us set aside our differences and be an answer to our Lord's prayer in John 17 for us to be one—that the world may know and experience his life-changing word and presence. This book tells us how to make this happen.

—DR. GARY KINNAMAN
Pastor, Author, and City Changer, Phoenix, AZ

IF IT WAS EASY

JESUS WOULDN'T
HAVE PRAYED FOR IT

HOW JESUS' STRATEGIC
PRAYER FOR UNITY
CAN REVOLUTIONIZE YOUR
CITY, CONGREGATION, AND HOME

DAVID DRUM

Adam Colwell's
writeworks

David Drum served as the solo/lead pastor of Community of Hope Lutheran Church from 1990–2011. In 2011 he started as the full time Church Domain Director for 4Tucson, helping churches and pastors throughout Tucson work more closely together. He is also the author of *Jesus' Surprising Strategy: A Mandate and a Means for City Transformation*, which has been published in English and Spanish. A Tucson, AZ native with a B.S. in Mechanical Engineering from the University of Arizona and an M.Div. from Trinity Lutheran Seminary, David and his wife Valerie have four children.

All Bible quotations, unless otherwise indicated, are from New International Version, 2011 (NIV 2011), copyright © 1973, 1978, 1984, 2011 by Biblica, Inc. Used by permission. All rights reserved worldwide.

Other Bible versions used are:
The Holy Bible, New Living Translation, copyright ©1996, 2004, 2007, 2013, 2015 by Tyndale House Foundation. Used by permission of Tyndale House Publishers, Inc., Carol Stream, Illinois 60188.
All rights reserved.

Adam Colwell's WriteWorks Publishing
Adam Colwell's WriteWorks LLC, Tucson, AZ
Copyright © 2017 by David Drum
All rights reserved. Published 2017
Printed in the United States of America

Edited by Adam Colwell
Cover Design and Typesetting by Cameron Hood
Cover Photo by Taylor Noel Photography
Author Photo by Rosaleen Ochoa

ISBN 978-0-9982593-7-6

CONTENTS

To my Lord and Savior Jesus Christ,
full of grace and truth. May your name become
the most famous name in our city.

FOREWORD

I am glad you picked up this book. Very soon, you will be, too.

I'd like to give you an invitation to come to Tucson, Arizona. Come, take a look—or actually, a read—at what God is doing. I have been there on several occasions and I can tell you that what you will read in these pages is not only true, it's transferable. What God has done in Tucson is unique. And what God is doing and wants to do in your city will also be unique. But you can learn, be encouraged, and inspired by Tucson's story.

In these pages, you will be able to meet with pastors from various backgrounds. Though their backgrounds are different, their future is the same. They have a growing common vision for what God wants to do in their city, and how each believer can find their place in that vision. You will be able to watch them work through some very sticky subjects. You will sit in on some staff meetings and prayer meetings that get uncomfortable. You will follow a guy around town who says—sometimes with a smile on his face, and sometimes with tears in his eyes—"my full-time job is to see John 17 answered across Tucson, AZ." You will be part of personal as well as public stories (some encouraging, some discouraging) to show the ongoing process of how Jesus is answering His own prayer through willing vessels in Tucson.

When I read Dave's first book, *Jesus' Surprising Strategy,* I knew he had many more valuable things to say on the topic of biblical unity and how it gets lived in the everyday, ordinary world. This book is proof that he did. He summarizes his primary point in the title, "If It Was Easy..."

The truth is, building and walking in unity in a city is not easy. If it was easy, Jesus would not have made it a key part of His passionate, John 17 prayer. If it was easy, we would see it happening far better in far more places. If it was easy, it would happen much more quickly. If it was easy...But there is not an "easy button" for this.

The questions in this book just might be worth the purchase price. Dave's use of questions act as "hooks" to take you further into a particular thought. In fact, this book not only contains many questions, it will cause you to ask some questions, too—such as, "How might Jesus' prayer for unity look in my town?" "What might my role be in what God wants to do?" "Would it be easier here than in Tucson?" And, "If it is not easy, is it still worth the hard work?"

So let's take a "read trip" to Tucson. Watch and listen. Wonder and ponder. Like I said earlier, you will be glad you did. Then you will be able to go back to your hometown and pray about what God may want to do there and how He may want to use you in the process.

—DENNIS FUQUA
Executive Director, International Renewal Ministries
www.prayersummits.net

Chapter One

UNITY: HOW TO GET IT ACCORDING TO JESUS

"IF it was easy, Jesus wouldn't have prayed for it." Those words frequently cross my lips these days. God graciously invited me to move from being a fan of John 17 to an employee of it—and it's the most thrilling ride of my life to date. Yet I've learned one thing for certain: if visible unity among Christians could happen by accident or as a byproduct of some other activity, Jesus would've focused His prayers elsewhere. Even more, if visible, citywide, substantive, Christ-centered unity was achievable through simple human effort and focus, the topic wouldn't have driven Jesus to His knees.

In these pages, I'll share insights gained from the inside as a John 17 employee privileged to connect to all the parts of the Tucson Body of Christ—the members of the City Church, all of the Christians in Tucson—while working alongside countless others to see the parts connect with one another. I'll also unpack the blessings that have emerged through unexpected trials, and I'll expand our understanding of exactly what is unity, how it works, and how we can draw even closer to Christ in the process.

Jesus' John 17 prayer is the furthest thing imaginable from a stream-of-consciousness laundry list. His prayer is strategic in every way. Three different times, Jesus specifically mentions what He's not praying, revealing how deliberate He was throughout. The setting was just as strategic: His entire three-year ministry came into focus right at the pivotal event in human history—the Son of God giving His life to redeem all humanity. At such a moment, we'd expect Jesus to be at the pinnacle of His focus and intentionality. I just wouldn't have ever guessed what He deemed most important.

Just over 40 days after that Thursday night, Jesus ascended back into Heaven and left the work of the Kingdom of God to be carried out by the Holy Spirit through broken human vessels. From my vantage point, that was the biggest gamble ever taken, with all future generations having to experience a human Body of Christ instead of the Divine One. Yet as contemporary Christian music artist Misty Edwards sings, "He knew what He was getting into when He called me."

What came into focus for Jesus mere hours before the cross is surely worthy of our attention, don't you agree? Even after six years of devoting my full-time attention to seeing Jesus' prayer answered in my city, His top priority—that we would be one—still staggers me.

HE TAUGHT MANY THINGS, BUT PRAYED ONE

If you have a red-letter edition of the Bible, it's apparent there was a lot on Jesus' mind the night before Good Friday. The Gospel of John chapters 13, 14, 15, 16, and 17 are all in red—almost entirely the words of Jesus with brief black-letter interruptions only when the disciples were confused about what Jesus was teaching. In chapters 13–16, Jesus taught on many topics. His first lesson started with an illustration that the disciples likely never forgot. If you didn't already know what follows these verses, you'd probably never guess:

> It was just before the Passover Festival. Jesus knew that
> the hour had come for him to leave this world and go

to the Father. Having loved his own who were in the
world, he loved them to the end. ²The evening meal was
in progress, and the devil had already prompted Judas,
the son of Simon Iscariot, to betray Jesus. ³Jesus knew
that the Father had put all things under his power, and
that he had come from God and was returning to God;
⁴so he . . . (John 13:1–4)

So He did what the rest of the disciples were too proud to do:
He took the role of the lowest of servants and washed the disciples'
feet. After that audacious and humble example, Jesus certainly could
have taught that the Church in generations to come would serve each
other, and a watching and unexpecting world, in the same way. In
fact, a unified and serving Body of Christ in Tucson has done more
to change the perception of the Christian Church in the city than
anything I could've ever imagined. He certainly could have prayed
that future leaders would understand that the only biblical model of
leadership is servant leadership. God knows we could benefit from
that lesson. Instead, Jesus turned His attention to the Holy Spirit,
saying that He is:

- A divine Counselor or Advocate (in the Greek, *paraclete*), literally the "called alongside one." (John 14:16)

- With us forever (John 14:16) and living within us (John 14:17)

- The Spirit of truth (John 14:17, 16:13) who teaches us all things
  and brings to mind Jesus' own words (John 14:26, 15:26)

- The One who convicts the world of guilt in regard to sin, righteousness, and judgment (John 16:7–11)

- The One who guides us into truth, revealing what we need to
  know about what's coming (John 16:13)

- The One who brings honor and glory to Jesus (John 16:14)

Undoubtedly, we need to be led by the Holy Spirit. If unity could be achieved outside of the Holy Spirit's empowering, Jesus could have settled for simply teaching on it. Yet His later prayer in John 17 didn't focus on our understanding of the Holy Spirit; it emphasized one of the outcomes of being led by the Holy Spirit—that we would be one even as Jesus is one with the Father.

Jesus also taught on the importance of obedience (John 14:21, 15:10), but obedience wasn't the subject of John 17. He taught to expect, anticipate, and endure persecution (John 15:18–16:4) and indeed is praying for us even now (Hebrews 7:25), but enduring persecution wasn't His prayer agenda later that evening. He taught that contrary to the popular opinion of our generation, there aren't many equal ways to God, but just one: Jesus, who is the way, the truth, and the life (John 14:6). Yet as confused as the world is on that one, Jesus didn't spend His evening calling for our clarity. He taught about the need for us to be as vitally connected to Him as branches are to the vine (John 15:1–8). He taught about how we can have peace (John 14:27, 16:33). He taught about Heaven (John 14:1–4) and even prayer itself (John 16:23–24). But He later prayed about none of those things extensively.

HIS TOP PRIORITY— THAT WE WOULD BE ONE— STILL STAGGERS ME.

Some parts of Christianity celebrate the climactic week of human history by calling it Holy Week, observing several specific days with special worship celebrations such as Palm Sunday, Maundy Thursday, Good Friday, and Easter Sunday. Maundy Thursday derives its name from the Latin word *mandate* and is taken from John 13:34–35: "A new command I give you: Love one another. As I have loved you, so you must love one another. 35By this everyone will know that you are my disciples, if you love one another." Among the many other Thursday evening lessons from the Master, Jesus taught that the world will come to notice our true identity as followers of Christ as we are one with each other and love one another well. This was clearly the pinnacle of His priorities, as He taught it again in John 15:12 and 15:17.

It was *this* command that was so critically important to Jesus that He not only taught it, He later prayed it.

And He's *still* praying it, for my city and for yours, for every believer in every place and every time. Hebrews 7:25 says, "He always lives to intercede for them." Hebrews 13:8 says, "Jesus Christ is the same yesterday, today, and forever." Put the two of those together, and we can make an educated guess what Jesus might be praying right now. But we don't have to guess, because as we'll see shortly, He tells us in this prayer that He's praying it continuously. For this reason, whenever I teach or write on John 17, I prefer to talk about the prayer in the present tense—because I believe it's a present tense prayer.

I've read John 17 for about 40 years. As a congregational pastor for over 20 of those years, I taught it multiple times, primarily applying it to the people in my congregation. Once I started working in a city-wide ministry, though, I noticed all kinds of gems I'd never unearthed before, particularly how incredibly descriptive Jesus was about the unity He taught and prayed for.

But it's been during the past year, when unity was tested at levels I'd never before experienced, that I also discovered how Jesus' own prayer for unity also contained the key for *achieving*, *maintaining*, and *maturing* that unity.

WHAT UNITY IS NOT TO BE

Many of the following descriptions are explored in greater depth in Chapter 1 of my previous book, *Jesus' Surprising Strategy*, but here they are in shorter detail as a refresher and primer for what's to come later in this book.

- *Unity is not uniformity* (John 17:11). Jesus prays that we would be one just as He is one with the Father. Jesus is clearly not identical with the Father—the most obvious difference being that at that moment the Father was an omnipresent spirit, while Jesus had taken on the limitations that come with being human.

The unity Jesus prays for is not one where all our differences are discounted or overlooked, but rather that we be completely aligned as different parts of one body. More insights on this topic will be shared in Chapter 3.

• *Unity is not private* (John 17:15). Jesus makes a point of mentioning that He isn't praying for us to be taken out of the world. The unity Jesus prays for must extend beyond the four walls of a congregation so that the world actually sees it in operation. This topic will be explored in greater depth in Chapter 6.

• *Unity is not watered down* (John 17:17). Right in the middle of Jesus' prayer for unity, He prays for us to be sanctified by the truth. The unity Jesus prays for is grounded in the truth of God's Word; it won't be achieved by overlooking or downplaying truth that seems inconvenient. Unity doesn't trump truth, but neither does truth undo unity. True unity is found in the truth, not around it. Chapter 8 grows out of this insight.

• *Unity is not just for the first century* (John 17:20). In another strategic statement, Jesus mentions that He was not only praying this content for the group of disciples gathered around Him in first century Palestine. This is His prayer for every generation in every locale. This is a universal prayer, a strategy that even imperfect human beings can use after Jesus had ascended back into Heaven.

• *Unity is not the end, but the means* (John 17:23). Unity itself isn't the ultimate purpose. The Church of Jesus Christ always has an outward focus; it's been said that the Church is the only organization to exist for its non-members. Even though Jesus had already pointed out that the unity He was praying for was public, not private, He comes full circle in His prayer. He reveals that the purpose of His wildly diverse believers being publicly and substantively united in every generation is so that the world would come to know the love of God.

BACK TO THE BEGINNING

The first six months of 2016 were the most challenging season I'd ever faced as an employee for John 17 in Tucson. 4Tucson, the very organization called to unite and mobilize the Body of Christ in Tucson, was threatening to implode. An incredibly promising program I'd worked on for more than two years was almost killed by a couple of ultimatums that were largely based on misunderstanding. Worst of all, I nearly became the detonator the enemy could use to blow it apart!

Back in 2009, Dennis Fuqua of International Renewal Ministries facilitated Tucson's first citywide Pastor Prayer Summit. That summit, itself the fruit of decades of laboring prayer warriors, changed the spiritual atmosphere in our city. An exceedingly diverse and isolated group of 20 pastors went up the mountain overlooking our city as individuals, but came down as a team. 4Tucson was officially born later that year—and we've had annual three-day Pastor Prayer Summits in the spring from then onward, adding one-day summits each fall in 2012. Dennis has facilitated each of the three-day summits.

In April of 2016, right in the middle of that tumultuous season for 4Tucson, we held our eighth three-day summit. Biblically, the eighth day is another way of saying the first day, back to the beginning. We had already asked Dennis in advance to also facilitate a time of prayer with our growing 4Tucson staff right after the time on the mountain with the pastors. In both settings, he ended up sharing a pattern in John 17 that I'd never seen exactly that way before. Here are Dennis' insights.

- Jesus made four petitions in John 17: glorify the Son, protect them from the enemy, sanctify them with the truth, and make them one.

- Each request is repeated; the request for unity shows up four times.

- In between the one or more times the petition is repeated, Jesus points out how He has personally experienced or achieved that exact petition.

Are you most passionate about prayer topics you've read about or those you're experiencing? It's no contest! I can go down a checklist and pray about a variety of topics that I believe are important, but if I'm in the middle of the battle while I'm on my knees, nobody has to encourage me to engage. I'm already there! I can pray about families in general, but I'll be "in the zone" if I'm praying about that morning's immediate challenges in my home. Most common-cause ministries[1] are birthed out of personal experience. What the enemy may have meant for evil God turns around for good. The very point of our deepest challenge becomes the source of our most powerful ministry. Jesus prayed for what He'd personally experienced, taught, and worked.

Because unity was being challenged so severely and personally at the very time Dennis shared these insights, the application was immediate. In the process of praying along with Jesus for unity instead of division, it became evident that the first three petitions are arguably the key components to that unity. This applies not just to unity at a citywide level in my day job, but it applies as well in my marriage, with my family, and in the local congregation.

HOW UNITY IS ACHIEVED: GLORIFYING THE SON

THE PATTERN:

- The first petition (John 17:1): "Father, the hour has come. Glorify your Son, that your Son may glorify you."

- The petition is repeated (John 17:5): "And now, Father, glorify me in your presence with the glory I had with you before the world began."

---

1   See Chapter 5 of *Jesus' Surprising Strategy.*

- Jesus prays from experience (John 17:4): "I have brought you glory on earth by finishing the work you gave me to do."

KEY INSIGHT:
Unity starts by glorifying Jesus.

In the Old Testament, the Hebrew word for "glory" brings with it the connotation of weight or substance—so to glorify Jesus is to acknowledge that Jesus has weight or substance. When unity has not yet been achieved between Christ-followers, or when unity was once present but is currently being threatened, it's likely that Jesus isn't being given the preeminent position He deserves.

"Putting Jesus first" means more than we think. I remember as a youth and later as a pastor attending multiple camps or retreats where we were given various prioritization exercises. "Your house is on fire and you can only take three things with you. What would you take?" or, "List the five things that are most important to you. Now imagine you're a refugee forcibly removed from your homeland. Cross off numbers 1, 3, and 5. How do you cope?" As Christians, we probably assume Jesus wants to be first on the list, or even that He deserves to be first. Yet that assumption is as erroneous as our compartmentalized culture. Jesus doesn't want to be first on your list—implying that there's a second, third, or fourth that is somehow distinct from the first. Jesus wants to be *the list!* He's preeminent over every item on it. He desires to touch, impact, and transform every aspect of our lives! More on this in Chapter 6.

> **JESUS' OWN PRAYER FOR UNITY ALSO CONTAINED THE KEY FOR ACHIEVING, MAINTAINING, AND MATURING THAT UNITY.**

When Christians of different flavors get together and "put Jesus first," it can easily mean that we're only going to talk about Jesus in ways that we're all comfortable with, using styles and languages familiar to everyone. That's far less than Jesus wants or intends. It's far better to connect with Jesus as He manifests Himself to us in each of the distinct languages, styles, and preferences of the gathered group. But that's far more challenging, too. In John 12:32, Jesus says, "And I, when I am lifted up from the earth, will draw all people to myself." He was literally referring to the cross, but was figuratively alluding to anytime He's glorified, lifted up, and given the weight and substance appropriate to the Lord of lords and King of kings. In every setting, the quest for unity starts by drawing closer to Jesus and lifting Him higher.

In marriage and family, much conflict can be minimized or eliminated by praying "glorify the Son." Genesis 22 contains the startling story of God asking Abraham to sacrifice his one and only son, Isaac. Pagan cultures of the day required child sacrifice; God was revealing Himself to His people, and Abraham had to learn how like or unlike these pagan religions his God was going to be. Isaac was the child of the promise. Abraham and Sarah were "as good as dead" (Hebrews 11:12) by the time they had their son Isaac. They had waited their entire lives, bearing the indignity of infertility. When Abraham and Sarah were 75 and 65 respectively, God promised they were going to have a son of their own. When the days and months turned to years and decades, the couple hatched a scheme to "help God along" with Abraham having a son through Sarah's maid, Hagar. Ishmael was born, but he was the child of presumption, not of promise. So by the time Isaac came along, the temptation to treat him with kid gloves and to in a sense "worship" him had to have been intense. "Give God the glory He deserves" was the message of Genesis 22. Abraham learned that God is in fact not like the other gods of the culture, and on his way down the mountain he also discovered that he could entrust his precious son Isaac to God in both dramatic and daily doses.

If we expect our spouse or family to "complete" us by providing our identity, purpose, and meaning, we're asking qualities from them they're simply not equipped to provide. They're bound to disappoint because they were never designed to carry attributes that belong to God alone. Acknowledging Jesus as the Alpha and the Omega, the beginning and the end, actually draws us closer to our family members. The best way to achieve unity with our family members is to have Jesus firmly in the center of it all; my wife and I are closer to one another when Jesus is completely in between us. Then when one of us blows it, we can point to Jesus in our weakness—and when we are weak, He is strong. Humility is at the very heart of glorifying Jesus, of declaring "there is a God, and it's not me!" Our failures can actually help us glorify Jesus, and unity will grow as a result.

In congregational or citywide unity, the exact same principles apply. When Jesus is acknowledged as the head of the body by all the parts of the body, it takes all the pressure off the body parts to look and act like one another. That isn't even the intention of the analogy. As parts of the Body of Christ, we aren't supposed to look and function alike, but are simply to take our directions from a common head, Jesus. As Gary Kinnaman shared at one of Glenn Barth's Good Cities Conferences in February, 2015, "Paul's solution in 1 Corinthians to the problem of disunity is 'to know nothing among you except Jesus Christ, and him crucified.' Jesus Christ plus nothing is our platform for unity. Whatever the something is that you add to Jesus becomes more important than Jesus."

For over four years now, African-American and Anglo pastors in Tucson have been meeting together every month. Apostle Warren Anderson of Living Water Ministries started the group with a question he posed to me: "Why is it that white Evangelicals seemed a lot more eager to pray for President Bush than they are to pray for President Obama?" That query birthed a Pastors Partnership group during the 2012 presidential election with the presenting question being, "Is our unity in Christ sufficient for us to be able to talk politics and live to tell about it?" The answer, thankfully, has been a resounding "yes," but that only happens when Jesus is intentionally glorified by everyone present. At the very first meeting, we agreed that we were going to address political issues not as Republicans or Democrats but as "Christocrats," followers of Jesus. It was even suggested that rather than anyone identifying themselves as the party of the elephant or the party of the donkey, we were all primarily the party of the Lamb. That's glorifying Jesus, giving Him the weight and substance He's earned—and that's the first step in unity. When Jesus is lifted up and draws all people to Himself, they're simultaneously drawn closer to one another.

QUESTION FOR SELF-REFLECTION

If you find yourself in the middle of conflict right now, ask yourself, "Am I acting in self-interest, or am I seeking to bring glory and honor to Jesus?" Seriously, stop reading until you've given the Holy Spirit permission to reveal any ways in which you're acting more selfishly than with the goal of glorifying the Son.

HOW UNITY IS MAINTAINED: PROTECTION FROM THE OUTSIDE

THE PATTERN:

- The first petition (John 17:11): "Holy Father, protect them by the power of your name, the name you gave me, so that they may be one as we are one."

- The petition is repeated (John 17:15): "My prayer is not that you take them out of the world but that you protect them from the evil one."

- Jesus prays from experience (John 17:12): "While I was with them, I protected them and kept them safe by the name you gave me."

KEY INSIGHT:

Unity is endangered by an enemy who seeks to divide and conquer.

Western culture is materialistic. It's not so much that we're focused on accumulating possessions (though that is also accurate) as it is that we're zeroed in on the material world that we can see. As a result, we easily overlook and even forget about the spiritual world, the reality that we cannot see. Other cultures have an easier time remembering this second petition than we do.

I recently preached a Sunday message on how these other three petitions help us achieve the unity that the rest of John 17 so aptly describes. During that time of intense attack on unity, I shared that if I forgot in the morning to put on the spiritual armor described in Ephesians 6:10–18, it was just a matter of time before I was pierced by the enemy's fiery darts. I'd start the day in great shape emotionally and spiritually, but within a few hours be convinced that I had to dramatically increase the anti-depressants I was taking—and was reminded anew that I was in a battlefield with a real and diabolical foe. On three different occasions over a two week stretch, the moment I remembered my oversight, I prayed, "Protect me from the enemy, Lord." Without fail, the cloud immediately lifted and I was strengthened and could see clearly how to fight the battles without being taken out by them. It was as dramatic an experience in spiritual warfare as I'd ever experienced. I shared that whole story in my message that Sunday, only to find that by Wednesday I had forgotten again! The sad truth is that I don't always take enemy fire when I forget; apparently, there are times that the enemy doesn't consider me a big enough threat to even warrant an attack. Yet every time I remembered and prayed, the conflicts that had so ominously threatened to take me out were approached with faith and confidence that the Son would indeed by glorified, and all was well.

We have an enemy whose chief strategy is to divide and conquer. This enemy is not flesh and blood, but spiritual and therefore never rests. Does Jesus pray for our protection from the enemy because Satan's chief strategy is to divide and conquer, or does Satan constantly seek to divide and conquer because Jesus prayed for unity? It's probably not either/or but both/and—as I'll address further in Chapter 8.

Every place where unity matters, the enemy is on the warpath. Is it any wonder that the family is under such intense assault as it is today in the United States of America? Likewise, congregations may experience seasons of unity where very little conflict is apparent, but if they're engaged in ministry and mission in significant ways, an attack on unity is on the horizon. In the City Church, brush fires of conflict ignited or fueled by the enemy are everywhere. How much more unity do you suppose the nation, congregations, or the City Church could experience if we all simply prayed regularly and fervently for God to protect us from Satan's insipid strategy to divide and conquer?

As if that's not serious enough, Revelation 12:10 says, "For the accuser of our brothers and sisters, who accuses them before our God day and night, has been hurled down." This is a reference to Satan, whose name literally means "accuser." He never rests in flinging about accusations, and the vast majority of the time he uses human mouthpieces! We want to be exceedingly cautious when dishing out allegations against fellow believers in our family, congregation, or the City Church because the devil is always looking for a new voice box. Self-proclaimed heresy hunters ought to be terrified by this verse and realize that their "ministry" to root out all error (as they see it) places them, at the very least, in alignment with Satan himself. Allowing Satan to spew accusations through our social media posts, emails, or phone calls is the furthest thing imaginable from the Ephesians 4:15 ideal of "speaking the truth in love."[2] One of the reasons the Christian Church in America remains so immature (the subject of Chapter 2) is that we rarely get close enough to one another to speak the truth in love out of a deeply committed relationship (the subject of Chapter 5). The goal is supposed to be humble reconciliation, not prideful one-upmanship.

> THE VERY POINT OF OUR DEEPEST CHALLENGE BECOMES THE SOURCE OF OUR MOST POWERFUL MINISTRY.

The truth is the Holy Spirit convicts but Satan condemns—always. The difference between the two is night and day. When the Holy Spirit speaks, it's to point out something that's amiss in order to drive us to the cross. The purpose is always hope-filled with healing, forgiveness, and resurrection the desired outcome. When Satan speaks, it's to keep

---

2   See Chapter 8 of *Jesus' Surprising Strategy.*

us from ever looking up to the cross and experiencing the joy and transformation of repentance. Satan's accusations aren't only against others; he's just as proficient in hurling his allegations personally. "You're hopeless. You'll always struggle with this. You're disqualified from all ministry. You should throw in the towel." Those are the words of the enemy whose goal is not healing, resurrection, and forgiveness from sin, but suffering, despair, and accommodation to sin. Be careful not to echo him when communicating with others.

Remember, the blood of Jesus has defeated Satan once and for all time. The ultimate outcome of the war is not in question. We know how the story ends. But Jesus' victory needs to be applied to every situation. When we resist the enemy, he flees (James 4:7). When we pray prayers of protection, Jesus is strong to be our Protector.

We need to be prayed up at all times, not just in seasons of conflict. Yet I find that if I pray the same thing over and over, I eventually check out mentally and lose focus. So I prayed Ephesians 6:10–18 during the early months of 2016 word for word.

> "Finally, be strong in the Lord and in his mighty power. ¹¹Put on the full armor of God, so that you can take your stand against the devil's schemes. ¹²For our struggle is not against flesh and blood, but against the rulers, against the authorities, against the powers of this dark world and against the spiritual forces of evil in the heavenly realms. ¹³Therefore put on the full armor of God, so that when the day of evil comes, you may be able to stand your ground, and after you have done everything, to stand. ¹⁴Stand firm then, with the belt of truth buckled around your waist, with the breastplate of righteousness in place, ¹⁵and with your feet fitted with the readiness that comes from the gospel of peace. ¹⁶In addition to all this, take up the shield of faith, with which you can extinguish all the flaming arrows of the evil one. ¹⁷Take the helmet of salvation and the sword

of the Spirit, which is the word of God. [18]And pray in the Spirit on all occasions with all kinds of prayers and requests. With this in mind, be alert and always keep on praying for all the Lord's people."

I then switched to 1 Corinthians 16:13–14, which says, "Be on your guard; stand firm in the faith; be courageous; be strong. [14]Do everything in love."

And more recently, I've been applying these three petitions to various aspects of my life. It's not a formula; it's a mindset. There's an enemy who wants to take us out. Act like you're in a battlefield—because you are.

QUESTION FOR SELF-REFLECTION
Do I act like I'm aware there's an enemy whose chief strategy is to divide and conquer? If I'm in the middle of conflict right now, am I particularly cautious before making accusations about others, knowing that accusations are Satan's first name?

HOW UNITY IS MATURED: PROTECTION FROM THE INSIDE

THE PATTERN:

- The first petition (John 17:17): "Sanctify them by the truth; your word is truth."

- The petition is repeated (John 17:19b): "...that they too may be truly sanctified."

- Jesus prays from experience (John 17:19a): "For them I sanctify myself..."

KEY INSIGHT:
Unity is endangered by our own sinfulness.

As cartoonist Walt Kelly said through his long-running comic strip, *Pogo*, "We've seen the enemy, and he is us." Another one of those questions that is both/and, not either/or, is, "Was that the enemy, or was that of human origin?" It's not a question of who's at fault, you or Satan, but discovering how both of you were likely involved.

To be sanctified means to be "set apart" or "made holy." The root *sanct* always has those connotations, as in sanctuary or sanctification. We can join Jesus in praying for God to sanctify us, purify us, and bring us more closely in line with God's plans and intentions for us. Sanctification is ultimately the work of the Holy Spirit, not something we can do for ourselves. But we have a role to play in cooperating and partnering with the Holy Spirit because He's unlikely to transform and mature us against our will. God's part/our part is the subject of Chapter 7.

Galatians 5:22–23 lists the fruit of the Spirit, those characteristics the Holy Spirit will produce in us to the extent that we allow. "The fruit of the Spirit is love, joy, peace, forbearance, kindness, goodness, faithfulness, 23gentleness and self-control." The first thing to notice is that "fruit" is singular, not plural. It's one fruit, one result of the Holy Spirit working in our lives to sanctify us. It's not a Holy Spirit supermarket where we can pick and choose. "I'll take five pounds of love, ten pounds each of joy and peace, but I'll pass on the self-control." Imagine the conflict avoided or permanently eliminated by believers who travel well down the sanctification road and are filled to overflowing with love, joy, peace, patience (another word for forbearance), kindness, goodness, faithfulness, gentleness and self-control? Wouldn't you guess that most or maybe *all conflict* is due to the absence of one or more of those qualities? Sanctify us, Lord! Fill us with more of your Holy Spirit fruit—for we are a fruit-starved people.

Today, there are far more people who self-identify as Christians who are not attending church than there are who are part of a congregation. In many cases, conflict is the reason: they once were a part of a congregation, but something painful happened to them within the church and they vowed not to go back. I like the way someone once addressed this reality. "If you ever find a perfect church, please don't join it, because you'll mess it up." If it wasn't for sinners, the Church would be out of business. The reason there's so much conflict in the world is because there are so many sinners!

We must remain diligent in striving for unity because what we learned yesterday isn't enough for today or tomorrow. Yesterday's food was used up yesterday; we need new food today. I believe sanctification is a lifelong process, meaning that this petition will be a lifelong prayer. At the beginning of Psalm 139, David says, "You have searched me, Lord, and you know me..." and he goes on to describe God's wonderful and powerful presence in great detail. By the end of the psalm, it's not a fact but a prayer: "Search me, God, and know my heart; test me and know my anxious thoughts. 24See if there is any offensive way in me, and lead me in the way everlasting." (Psalm 139:23–24) Once again, the Holy Spirit's conviction is the furthest thing possible from the enemy's condemnation. We can approach the throne of grace with boldness and confidence (Hebrews 4:16) because anything the Spirit sanctifies in us will be an improvement! I bring myself to every conflicted situation, so praying for God to sanctify me is always wise. Not only will I benefit, but so will everyone around me.

QUESTION FOR SELF-REFLECTION
Am I growing and maturing in the fruit of the Holy Spirit? Do I have testimonies of this that are recent, not back from when I first came to know the Lord? What can I identify that the Lord has changed within me from last year? Last month? Last week?

If unity was easy, Jesus wouldn't have prayed for it. John 17 tells us that He not only prayed for it, but that it's what He was praying right before He gave His life for us on the cross. His prayer gives us tremendous insight on what unity looks like. But Jesus' prayer also gives us a pattern for how we can join Him in His own prayer and see unity happen where we need it the most—in our marriages and families, in our congregations, and in our City Church. "Help me glorify Jesus in my current circumstances. Protect me from the enemy. Sanctify me." It's such a simple pattern for achieving something so difficult that it drove the Son of God to His knees.

This pattern has become my literal GPS for most days, both with the challenges I face at home and the challenges I face through my profession: Glorify the Son, Protect me/us from the enemy, Sanctify me/us with your truth. These three simple GPS petitions are helping me avoid many conflicts, and guiding me through those that can't be or weren't avoided. Praying with Jesus is transformational. Praying John 17 in this way is daily changing my life at multiple levels.

In the next chapter, we'll look at the tremendous competition brewing between which group of people needs Jesus' John 17 strategy the most.

Today's GPS

God, we join You in praying what Jesus Himself prayed as He went to His knees for our unity. In my marriage and with my children, would You help all of us to glorify Jesus and give Him the centrality He deserves? Reveal any areas where my own unresolved wounds could have me act in self-interest rather than glorifying Jesus. In our homes, congregations, and City Church, protect us from the enemy who seeks to divide and defeat us. Help us catch him when he tempts us to be his mouthpiece of accusation, and protect our homes, congregations, and City Church from our own sinfulness. When we fail, which we will, help us to glorify You by running to Your cross in humility and receiving Your grace and forgiveness. Sanctify and mature us, and fill us with the fruit of Your Holy Spirit. May we be brought to such complete unity that the world around us comes to know Your never-ending and limitless love. Amen.

Chapter Two

MATURITY: IT'S MORE SERIOUS THAN WE THOUGHT

IF maturity was easy to attain, we'd have to call it something else. The very word implies that it's going to take time and effort. There's no quick fix, no "five simple steps to maturity." It takes a broad range of experiences over a significant chunk of time to travel very far down the road marked maturity.

There are two groups of people who need Jesus' prayer in John 17 to be answered: us and them. Them—those who are not yet followers of Jesus—need to see the Body of Christ, people so different from one another that only Jesus could bring them together, united visibly. According to John 17:23, that's how the world will come to know the love of God and the identity of Jesus. Remember, since Jesus incarnate ascended to Heaven, we're the Body of Christ left visible on Earth. That truth places an astonishing urgency on the essence of our unity. How well my city comes to know the love of God and person of Jesus depends on how truly united our City Church is and remains. This is vitally important.

But it's even more serious than that! Not only does the world need the Body of Christ to unite, so does the Body of Christ! Our maturity as believers grows out of our own unity. I didn't know or believe that five years ago, but now I believe it because I've seen it—not only in how it plays out in one person after another, but in how that truth is taught time and again in the New Testament. When Jesus prayed, "Sanctify them by the truth; your word is truth," (John 17:17) I think He was also praying for the maturity He taught in various ways earlier in the evening.

Do we take unity as seriously as Jesus does? Do we value what Jesus values? Do we pray and work for what Jesus prays and works?

THE WORLD ISN'T THE ONLY GROUP WHO NEEDS A UNIFIED BODY OF CHRIST; CHRISTIANS DO, TOO.

Most congregations of more than a few dozen people will divide up responsibilities in some manner or another to make sure that the most important things don't get overlooked. Perhaps elders or deacons are assigned specific tasks; maybe it's a committee or team designated to keep their eye on that ball. As a congregation grows, staff may be hired to ensure that not only are the volunteers paying attention, but the paid staff who can more easily be held accountable are paying attention, too, so that no priorities get sidelined.

Congregations acknowledge many priorities: pastoral care, discipleship, evangelism, small groups, worship, missions, outreach, hospitality, facilities, and more. Subgroups are identified and highlighted: children and families, youth, young adults, singles, married couples, seniors, and more. We recognize the need to not leave anything or anyone out. Sometimes entirely new denominations, networks, or movements have sprung up because people whose hearts break with the things that break the heart of God[1] have rightfully noticed a missing piece to the way Christ followers are following Christ.

---

1   As Robert Pierce, founder of World Vision, is quoted.

Have we overlooked the one priority that drove Jesus to His knees on the eve of the cross? Often the "bring the pieces together" puzzle piece is the one piece that gets lost. Few congregations I'm aware of have a staff position, committee/team, or elder/deacon devoted to citywide unity. I don't know many congregations, networks, or denominations that have dedicated one person to the primary responsibility of seeing Jesus' prayer answered because it's the one "wildly important goal" that can't get crowded out by the "whirlwind."[2]

The danger inherent to making someone responsible for a particular focal point is that the rest can assume "that's their job" and feel good about personally ignoring the topic. That danger is why one of the most commonly used passages in the New Testament on leadership and church structure is Ephesians 4. There we learn that the purpose of leadership isn't to do the work, but to equip the *Body of Christ* to do the work. I'm now convinced the main point of this text could actually be something else.

THE MOST POWERFUL EXPERIENCE OF MY LIFE TO DATE

In Chapter 1, I referenced a promising 4Tucson program that took place in 2016 that was nearly ended before ever seeing the light of day. It was conceived three years earlier when a non-staff, non-clergy follower of Christ, Dave Strong, came to me with an idea. I first met Dave through some "citywide" retreats known as Via de Cristo weekends. "Citywide" is in quotes because it brought together people from more than one congregation, but only from within Lutheran circles—and even that is stretching it, because it only brought together the Lutherans most like one another. Via de Cristo, Walk to Emmaus, and Cursillo are all very similar, intense, and highly structured three-day weekends where the gospel is experienced and taught while Christian community is built and nurtured. I've worked on a few dozen weekends for both adults and teens since 1994, and all have been powerful experiences.

Dave's idea was to bring another expression, Tres Dias, to Tucson. While Cursillo, Via de Cristo, and Walk to Emmaus all tend to bring

---

2   The terms used by McChesney, Covey, and Huling in their book, *The 4 Disciplines of Execution.*

people together from a particular denomination, Tres Dias intentionally brings people together from multiple theological backgrounds. The two weekend events, one for men and the other for women, are thoroughly Christian and focused on Jesus, so they're not "interfaith" but rather an expression of the kind of unity Jesus prays for. Another gift of the weekends is that the way they're structured does an excellent job of raising up, training, and equipping servant leaders. A typical leadership team of 50 will only have two to five pastors, with everyone else being a layperson. By the end of my 20-plus year tenure as pastor of a Lutheran church in Tucson, nearly 70 percent of my leaders had been through one of the Lutheran Via de Cristo weekends—not because it was a requirement, but simply because it was a valuable tool we were happy to promote.

I was immediately interested in Tres Dias since one of the most common requests the past few years from area pastors had been, "How can we help our congregations experience this same John 17 unity that we've been experiencing in our Prayer Summits and monthly gatherings?" I knew this could be a significant part of the answer to that question.

But I was also immediately cautious. By that point I'd been working with 4Tucson for a couple of years. We'd experienced more progress in bringing the Body of Christ together than I anticipated, crossing ethnic and generational lines as well as denominational ones. If we were going to offer Tres Dias in Tucson, a non-negotiable for me was that it truly represented the entire Body of Christ in our city. "I don't want this culturally to be a white Lutheran weekend that we ask everyone else to assimilate into," I said to Dave bluntly. "The Christian community that gets built has to reflect the whole Body of Christ." Dave Strong to this day phrases it this way: "This can't be a gathering of OWLS— Old White Lutherans."

A second concern is the petition Jesus prays in John 17 to protect us from the enemy. Any time a powerful tool is raised up in the Body of Christ, Satan goes to work distorting it. There's nothing unique about the weekends themselves; they're simply the gospel being lived out in an environment free from outside distractions. One of the enemy's most effective weapons is getting us to focus on the tool itself, the gift, instead of the Giver behind it. The more powerful the tool, the more likely the enemy is to tempt us to turn it into an idol, as per the discussion about Abraham and Isaac in Chapter 1. This three-day weekend culture has become "the church" for some. They have found the weekends so powerful that insider/outsider language has developed, epitomized by comments like, "You may think you're a follower of Christ now, but you haven't seen anything until you've joined the club."[3] Tres Dias weekends could easily become one more tool the enemy abuses to divide the Body of Christ in Tucson.

Finally, the calendar of City Church activities in Tucson is substantial. After the weekends are completed, subsequent (often monthly) reunions of people who've experienced a particular three-day weekend have been part of the culture around the country and world. While there's value in that, especially if there's nothing else like it available, I wanted to be sure that our weekends didn't compete with the work that God was already doing in Tucson, but rather flow out of it and then flow back into it with renewed vigor. I'm as competitive as the next guy, but the last thing I wanted was more events competing with each other for the City Church's attention.

It took us a year and a half working with the national leadership of Tres Dias to become convinced that this could work without us having to reinvent the wheel and start from scratch—so work we did. We scheduled the weekends for July 2016 and started promoting them, building the teams, and recruiting our participants. One significant segment of the Body of Christ in Tucson, however, considered not participating because of the weekends' historic ties to the Catholic Church. The basic flow and format of the weekends were originally developed in the 1940's in Spain by some Catholic lay people who wanted to help men renew their faith and truly follow Christ in everyday life. While the content we were using had no current ties to the Catholic Church, the historic connection was enough to raise serious concerns. There were multiple

---

3   See chapter 5 of *Jesus' Surprising Strategy* for more on this topic.

conversations dealing with the conflict, and after each one, I thought we had resolution, only to find the conflict even larger in the next conversation. In the middle of unity being threatened on every front, it looked like I was going to have to choose between either moving forward with this program without a major section of the Body of Christ (a non-option for me from the beginning) or abandoning it in order to keep the peace.

One of the key leaders of the concerned group is a person that I met at the very first Pastor Prayer Summit in Tucson and have grown closer to every year since then. Our commitment to one another is substantial (see Chapter 5 for the significance of this), enabling us to truly speak the truth in love to one another, even when it hurt. A final pivotal conversation carried with it very real possibilities that Satan might successfully tempt us to claim irreconcilable differences. Instead, through much mutual prayer, commitment to unity, and tough conversation, we agreed to proceed with the weekends as planned, and my friend and colleague committed to have someone from their group attend, check it out, and provide feedback. In turn, I promised him that we would look at every part of the experience and evaluate it after the weekends were over. I also committed that we would not hold a second round of weekends until we had adjusted anything that needed to be changed and had gained their full enthusiastic support. We're better together!

> AN ISOLATED AND SEPARATED BODY OF CHRIST, LET ALONE A BICKERING ONE, WILL NEVER REPRESENT THE WHOLE MEASURE OF THE FULLNESS OF CHRIST.

The weekends took place—despite the enemy's overtime work right until the program started. It was uncanny how many people were tempted right up until the last minute to drop out and not attend. That is always the case to some degree on these weekends, but I had never seen anything even close to the extent that it happened this time. We had 25 congregations send participants, and the concerns raised by my dear friend helped us eliminate some potential stumbling blocks along the way. The team that helped make this first set of weekends a reality came from all over Arizona and even a couple of surrounding states. When Phoenix, AZ residents (suburb Tempe, AZ is home of the Arizona State University Sun Devils) and people who live in Tucson (home of the University of Arizona Wildcats) work together, you know God is in the house.

The two John 17 Weekends, one with 70 men followed by another with 70 women (plus three male pastors), were the most powerful experiences I've ever had—and I don't say that lightly. For the next 40 days after the weekends, not a single day passed without someone telling me how dramatically it had impacted their life. One Millennial woman said, "It was ridiculous, in a good way. I came to a place where I'm content with who God created me to be." Heart transformations that I've personally prayed for over many years happened for me, too, and are still growing today. A large number of the attendees experienced deep healing physically, spiritually, and relationally, and many more people from the weekends are now fully engaged in the City Church work in Tucson.

The world ("them") isn't the only group who need a unified body of Christ; Christians ("us") do, too. A unified Body of Christ not only benefits the onlookers Jesus prayed would be impacted, it also deeply impacts the Body itself, bringing it closer and closer to God's intention and design. I spent a lot of time during and since the John 17 Weekends reflecting on what made the experiences so powerful. Here's what I found from God's Word.

MATURITY IS AN OUTGROWTH FROM UNITY: EPHESIANS 4

Verses 11–16 are the heart of Ephesians 4, and it is the passage that congregational leaders often turn to for training and implementing leadership structures in their congregations. Let's take that section verse by verse, and then discuss what comes before and after it.

- *Verse 11:* "So Christ himself gave the apostles, the prophets, the evangelists, the pastors and teachers..." These five terms are understood in widely divergent ways across the Body of Christ. Some see them as spiritual gifts, others as congregational positions, and still others as citywide roles. Some groups use the terms as titles or offices, while others don't even recognize some of the terms as applicable, modern-day realities. I had some knowledge of this ten years ago, but the last six years working full-time across the city has broadened my appreciation for the diversity of the usage of this terminology. In addition, I don't know of any congregation, network, or denomination that excels at all five equally. Is that a problem? Only if we fail to remember that the starting point when you think "church" in the New Testament is the city, not any subgroup smaller than that. This point is fully developed in *Jesus' Surprising Strategy*, Chapter 2.

- *Verse 12:* "...to equip his people for works of service, so that the body of Christ may be built up..." Regardless of the specifics of how the five terms in verse 11 are understood, it's clear that their purpose is not self-serving, but to build up and equip the Body of Christ. This is one of the hardest concepts to maintain for leaders: their responsibility isn't to get the job done themselves, but to equip others to get the job done. Most people I know, myself included, enter some aspect of ministry because they love doing that facet of ministry; it's counter-intuitive that our role is to work ourselves out of a job. Is there any indication in this verse that anything less than the entire citywide Body of Christ is in mind? Not that I can see. The purpose of these gifts/roles/offices which are spread out across the body is to ensure that the entire body, with all its distinct parts, gets built up. To what extent?

- *Verse 13:* "...until we all reach unity in the faith and in the knowledge of the Son of God and become mature, attaining to the whole measure of the fullness of Christ." There it is! Maturity grows out of unity. Unity is expressed both in faith (a more relational term) and knowledge (a more intellectual term). Both relational maturity and intellectual maturity are the goal. And to what extent is the unified Body of Christ supposed to mature? "The whole measure of the fullness of Christ." When people see the earthly, present-day Body of Christ, they're supposed to see Christ Himself. That will never happen with the body separated into pieces; it only happens with the body as a whole. An isolated and separated Body of Christ, let alone a bickering one, will never represent the whole measure of the fullness of Christ.

The next three verses expound on verse 13.

- *Verse 14:* "Then we will no longer be infants, tossed back and forth by the waves, and blown here and there by every wind of teaching and by the cunning and craftiness of people in their deceitful scheming." The concept of maturity is developed by referencing its opposite, infancy. In infancy, we haven't yet learned how to stand firm, literally or figuratively. There's emotional infancy, where the slightest wind of difficulty can knock us off kilter, and there's intellectual infancy, where we can't distinguish truth from error and believe anything we see or hear. In both cases, the picture used here is that if you stand alone, it's easier to get knocked over, but when you stand together, you're much more solid. You can support each other, and "better together" also means greater maturity. How's this for a takeaway that would probably generate plenty of conversation among denominational theologians (whether in a non-denominational denomination or a named one): unity isn't in contrast to right doctrine; it's the only way to achieve it. Author and speaker Derek Prince put it this way: "When you tell me what denomination you're a part of, all you've really told me is what truth you've stopped at."[4]

- *Verse 15:* "Instead, speaking the truth in love, we will grow to become in every respect the mature body of him who is the

---

4   I heard this through Pastor Isaac Martinez, who attributed it to Prince. A quick search couldn't help me locate the source.

head, that is, Christ." Could it be any clearer? We need enough depth of relationship that we can have the courage to point out one another's blind spots, and receive with gratitude the same gift from others who are pointing out our *own* blind spots. The definition of a blind spot is "when we don't know what we don't know." We need relationships with people in the Body of Christ who are different enough from us that they likely have strengths and weaknesses different than ours. That's the best way for blind spots to be discovered. In Luke 6:32, Jesus said, "If you love those who love you, what credit is that to you? Even sinners love those who love them." We need to learn to love those who, apart from Jesus, we'd likely never even meet.

At the Willow Creek Global Leadership Summit in 2015, Bill Hybels gave a talk on blind spots. Typically, after each of the global leadership summits, one of the talks generates the most buzz around the city, and his was the one that year. The Christian community isn't the only one talking about blind spots: "What counts for most people in investing is not how much they know, but rather how realistically they define what they don't know."[5] Left unaddressed, our blind spots make us part of the problem instead of part of the solution. Our isolation and our proclivity to hang out with those most like ourselves is what has kept

> UNITY ISN'T IN CONTRAST TO RIGHT DOCTRINE; IT'S THE ONLY WAY TO ACHIEVE IT.

the Body of Christ so immature. The political climate in the United States leading up to the 2016 presidential election was one of the most sobering indications I can imagine for how immature the body of Christ has become since we're supposed to be the salt, light, and leaven for our culture. More on this topic in Chapter 4.

---

5   Warren Buffett, *The Oracle of Omaha.*

- *Verse 16:* "From him the whole body, joined and held together by every supporting ligament, grows and builds itself up in love, as each part does its work." Could it be any clearer? Did I say that already? This is talking about the whole body, not any subset of it. What a powerful picture of the citywide Body of Christ—and it's exactly what we experienced at the retreats when the entire body came together for 72 uninterrupted hours with Jesus—clergy and laity who were ethnically, denominationally, generationally, and geographically diverse. The power of the retreats came from the whole body growing and building itself up in love as each part of the body did its work.

Allow me to diagram Ephesians 4:11–16 this way: the goal is for the Body of Christ to resemble Christ Himself. Verse 13 states this goal in the highest possible terms as the measure of the stature of the fullness of Christ, as the NASB translates it. The world needs Christians to look like Christ, and so do Christians. Immediately before and after the Mt. Everest phrase "the measure of the stature of the fullness of Christ" is the topic of spiritual maturity. Earlier in verse 13, the word "mature" is used; immediately after, in verses 14–15, immaturity is described as something to be avoided. Then, right before and after maturity is addressed, we find the topic of unity: in verse 13 it's named, and in verse 16 it's powerfully pictured. Unity in the Body of Christ is how maturity in the Body of Christ is achieved.

Ephesians 4:17–32 provides incredibly practical instructions on how to unify in every setting. I attended a Navigator Bible Camp after college that employed the rule based on Ephesians 4:29 to "not let anything unhelpful come out of your mouth, but only words that build up." Many brides and grooms have been taught Ephesians 4:26 in their premarital counseling or wedding homilies: "don't let the sun go down while you are still angry." "In your anger, do not sin" (verse 26) lets us know that anger isn't the problem: there are things that ought to make us angry. It's what we do with our anger that determines whether we're being faithful or faithless. Several of the fruit of the Spirit discussed in Chapter 1 show up in this passage. The entire section illuminates Jesus' prayer, "Sanctify them by the truth; your word is truth." (John 17:17) If we back up to the sections that precede Ephesians 4:11–16, verse 7 sets the stage for the five gifts/roles/offices in verse 11: "But to each one of us grace has been given as Christ apportioned it." The language is similar to 1 Corinthians 12, where Paul develops the analogy of the body with many parts. Each one of the five gifts/roles/offices is an expression of grace from a gracious God, and each is designed to build up the entire body together.

Ephesians 4:3 says, "Make every effort to keep the unity of the Spirit through the bond of peace." That's the theme for this book! If it was easy, Jesus wouldn't have prayed for it. It's worth the effort, though, because if we keep at it, aligning ourselves with Jesus' John 17 prayer, glorifying the Son, praying for protection from the enemy, and pursuing sanctification from sinful selves, we'll be able to join together in singing the great song of unity that is Ephesians 4:4–6—and was likely an early hymn at the time Paul penned it: "There is one body and one Spirit, just as you were called to one hope when you were called; ⁵one Lord, one faith, one baptism; ⁶one God and Father of all, who is over all and through all and in all."

The beginning of Ephesians 4 reminds us again why this unity business is more serious than we thought. "As a prisoner for the Lord, then, I urge you to live a life worthy of the calling you have received." Given where the rest of the chapter goes, I don't think it's a stretch to say that aligning ourselves with Jesus' own prayer priorities is essential to live a life worthy of the calling we have received. It's not, "If unity happens, great, but if not, oh well." No, it's "make every effort!" Unity isn't optional! If we aren't investing in unity, we're purchasing immaturity.

Finally (and significantly), Ephesians 4:2 contains the single word that determines whether or not we'll stay isolated or make the effort to unify. "Be completely humble and gentle; be patient, bearing with one another in love." Humility is the key. I wrote at the beginning of Chapter 7 of *Jesus' Surprising Strategy,* "True love for one another will go only as far as humility takes it. We can set aside our differences with only a minimal amount of humility. We can come to appreciate our differences with large doses of humility. We can break through the barriers our differences will inevitably create only if humility becomes a significant character trait... Pride is the greatest barrier to true love for one another, and humility the greatest fuel." *All* of my experiences of the last six years have confirmed the truth of those statements.

HEALING IS AN OUTGROWTH FROM UNITY: JAMES 5

The last night of the John 17 Weekends featured healing and reconciliation opportunities around the cross. Jesus' love had been so evident in the previous two days that nobody had to encourage anyone to lay down their burdens, shame, and sin at the cross—we just had to get out of the way so no one was trampled! I shared a couple of verses from James 5.

> "Is anyone among you in trouble? Let them pray. Is anyone happy? Let them sing songs of praise. [14]Is anyone among you sick? Let them call the elders of the church to pray over them and anoint them with oil in the name of the Lord. [15]And the prayer offered in faith will make the sick person well; the Lord will raise them up. If they have sinned, they will be forgiven. [16]Therefore confess your sins to each other and pray for each other so that you may be healed. The prayer of a righteous person is powerful and effective." (James 5:13–16)

The "anoint them with oil," "prayer offered in faith," and "confess your sins to each other" parts were all familiar, and I was eager to see how it was going to be implemented in such a diverse setting where each group's familiarity with those actions differed greatly. What struck me in the moment, though, was the "call the elders of the church" part. The book of James is clearly not written to a single congregation, and as we've already seen, "church" in the New Testament usually refers to a citywide church made up of multiple congregations.[6] That's who were

---

6   That's also why I typically use "church" for citywide expressions and "congregation" for local expressions.

present that evening: leaders from the City Church! It's no wonder, then, the level of healing was closer to scriptural standards than I'd ever seen; the gathering itself resembled the citywide church of the New Testament.

Keeping with the theme of "it's more serious than we thought," James wrote just a few verses earlier, "Don't grumble against one another, brothers and sisters, or you will be judged." (James 5:9) Do we prefer healing or judgment?

MATURITY IS AN OUTGROWTH FROM UNITY: HEBREWS 6

I've recently discovered more passages in the New Testament that also speak to maturity and unity in the same way as Ephesians 4. One caught my attention a few months after the John 17 Weekends. Hebrews is another book that's clearly addressed to an audience larger than a single congregation. The beginning of chapter six is entirely focused on the topic of maturity and immaturity. "Therefore let us move beyond the elementary teachings about Christ and be taken forward to maturity." (Hebrews 6:1) The text continues by giving some examples of elementary teachings as well as a vexing warning about immature living. But notice how the author continues the discussion:

> "God is not unjust; he will not forget your work and the love you have shown him as you have helped his people and continue to help them. [11]We want each of you to show this same diligence to the very end, so that what you hope for may be fully realized. [12]We do not want you to become lazy, but to imitate those who through faith and patience inherit what has been promised." (Hebrews 6:10–12)

UNITY ISN'T OPTIONAL! IF WE AREN'T INVESTING IN UNITY, WE'RE PURCHASING IMMATURITY.

Hebrews links maturity to loving God and loving (uniting with) one another.

MATURITY IS AN OUTGROWTH FROM UNITY: COLOSSIANS 2

I read another passage the day after the first men's John 17 Weekend as part of my devotional time in the New Living Translation. It was like somebody had turned on the light for the first time.

> "I want you to know how much I have agonized for you and for the church at Laodicea, and for many other believers who have never met me personally. [2]I want them to be encouraged and knit together by strong ties of love. I want them to have complete confidence that they understand God's mysterious plan, which is Christ himself. [3]In him lie hidden all the treasures of wisdom and knowledge. [4]I am telling you this so no one will deceive you with well-crafted arguments. [5]For though I am far away from you, my heart is with you. And I rejoice that you are living as you should and that your faith in Christ is strong. [6]And now, just as you accepted Christ Jesus as your Lord, you must continue to follow him. [7]Let your roots grow down into him, and let your lives be built on him. Then your faith will grow strong in the truth you were taught, and you will overflow with thankfulness. [8]Don't let anyone capture you with empty philosophies and high-sounding nonsense that come from human thinking and from the spiritual powers of this world, rather than from Christ. [9]For in Christ lives all the fullness of God in a human body. [10]So you also are complete through your union with Christ, who is the head over every ruler and authority."

Verse 2 ties unity and maturity together as the theme for Paul's entire line of reasoning. As you read through the rest of Colossians 2, you'll see that this thread continues, dealing with the themes of maturity and immaturity, and you'll notice how central to achieving maturity is our connection to both the Head and to one another.

MATURITY IS AN OUTGROWTH FROM UNITY: PRESBYTERIANS

Okay, that's somewhat tongue in cheek, but it does spring from a real story. A particularly city-minded Presbyterian Church hosted the John 17 Weekends and was not only incredibly gracious and generous, but actually thrilled for the opportunity. Lead pastor Jim Toole was taking a sabbatical the summer of 2016, so he put together a sermon series called, "Deep Church, Deep Faith," and invited several of us city pastors to each take a Sunday to teach. I immediately signed up for the Sunday right before the John 17 Weekends. At the beginning of my message, I read off the list of the 25 congregations who were sending representatives to the weekends, and spontaneous applause broke out. Depending on your background, that might not seem noteworthy, but let me assure you that spontaneous applause in the middle of a mainline sermon in a primarily Anglo congregation in the United States is about as frequent as snow days in the Sonoran Desert.

I then proceeded to share some of the points from this chapter and concluded by summarizing Richard Foster from his book, *Streams of Living Water: Celebrating the Great Traditions of the Christian Faith*. Whole denominations and cultures tend toward one or the other of these streams. Is that a problem? Only if the streams are kept isolated from one another. It's a great read that I encourage you to check out, but I'll summarize his section headings here along with some brief commentary.

- *The Contemplative Tradition: Discovering the Prayer-Filled Life.* Prayer is a declaration of dependence on God. What would our Christianity be if we operated within our own power, as if God was mostly unnecessary or merely locked in history? But let's be honest: some parts of the Body of Christ are much more mature in their prayer development than others, and all of us could learn something from the different styles of prayer exercised in different parts of the body.

- *The Holiness Tradition: Discovering the Virtuous Life.* Foster points out that the purpose of the holiness tradition is not to get us into Heaven, but to get Heaven into us. Character transformation is desperately needed in our day, and judgment starts with the house of God (1 Peter 4:17). You may have noticed the bumper stickers that read, "Jesus I like, it's His followers I can't stand." Who needs John 17 unity? Us and them.

- *The Charismatic Tradition: Discovering the Spirit-Empowered Life.* Foster calls this an ongoing correction to our impulse to domesticate God. It's been a tremendous blessing in our experiences in the City Church in Tucson to have Charismatic, Pentecostal, and Evangelical streams flowing together. Spiritual gifts, spiritual fruit, and signs and wonders all dot the pages of the New Testament. For those in the Evangelical tradition who hold to a high view of Scripture, how can we ignore the authority of parts of it? When God confronted me with the realization that I was taking parts of the Scriptures very seriously while conveniently ignoring other parts, my faith matured as a result.

- *The Social Justice Tradition: Discovering the Compassionate Life.* This tradition bridges personal ethics with social ethics, and is so important and often so isolated that I've devoted a chapter to it (Chapter 4). This topic isn't limited to cross cultural partnerships, but that's the place where I've learned the most about it.

- *The Evangelical Tradition: Discovering the Word-Centered Life.* While the social justice tradition helps remind us that God cares greatly about life on Earth, the Evangelical tradition keeps us from forgetting that eternity matters, too! When Jesus prayed, "Sanctify them by the truth; your word is truth," He was helping us in future generations see the role the written Word of God can play in making it easier to discern truth from error. Each part of the Body of Christ develops expertise in different parts of the Word, which is why we so desperately need one another.

- *The Incarnational Tradition: Discovering the Sacramental Life.* The incarnational tradition reveals that God is truly among us, not distant or disinterested. Does that sound like a message the world is hungry to hear? While not limited to Sacraments such as Baptism and Communion, how we handled Sacraments was a sensitive area for the John 17 Weekends. What Jesus instituted to unite us the enemy has twisted into a major source of division. While this is an oversimplification, when it comes to Communion, some parts of the body emphasize the "this is my body" and "this is my blood" portions of Jesus' words, while other parts emphasize the "do this in remembrance of me" portion of His words. Do we have to choose one over the other? Can't we respect one another, learn from one another, and grow in love for one another until we can experience the full measure of the whole body of Christ?

IF THE VARIOUS STREAMS ARE KEPT SEPARATE, SHALLOW FAITH RESULTS.

Since the topic of the sermon series was "Deep Church, Deep Faith," I pointed out the obvious but sadly underemphasized point: These streams are shallow by definition. If the various streams are kept separate, shallow faith results (a concept developed further in upcoming chapters). But when the streams come together, a mighty river results, and the whole dusty, dry desert city comes to know the love of God.

If all the streams came together—if our unity was made perfect, as some translations render John 17:23—I'm convinced that even if the entire world came to know the love of God as a result, we'd still find Jesus praying the same prayer because unity is the believers' path to maturity. We ("us") need it as much or more than they ("them") do.

John 17 teaches us what unity is and isn't, what unity does (show the world the love of God), and how unity happens. The Apostle Paul developed Jesus' prayer into a citywide analogy that continues to function like treasure hidden in a field, resulting in surprising new discoveries along the way. In the next chapter, we'll take a look at how a simple change in translation of a common biblical text on unity is unlocking whole new vistas of understanding and application of Paul's analogy.

QUESTIONS FOR SELF-REFLECTION

- What would it mean for your congregation to have someone responsible for citywide unity who is equipping the rest of the congregation to join in as well? It can't be the lead pastor, though it's certainly best if the lead pastor is fully involved and supportive. (If you live in Tucson, please be sure to contact me and tell me who that person is; we have a lot of work to do together, and this has been one of the two or three greatest hurdles we've yet to overcome.)

- Do you believe that "if you're not investing in unity, you're purchasing immaturity?" How's your investment portfolio doing? Is it growing? Flatlined? In a recession? Or non-existent?

- What blessings have you personally experienced from developing relationships with sisters and brothers in Christ who are very different from you?

TODAY'S GPS

Precious Jesus, we honor You as King of kings and Lord of lords. You are the head of Your body on Earth, the Church, and Your position is not threatened. From Your position of authority, You prayed that we would become one as You and the Father are one—not only so that the world would notice and come to know Your true identity, but also so that we ourselves would grow up into Your full stature. Protect us from the deceiver who convinces us so frequently that we don't need one another, or that our vantage point is purer than others' is, or that isolation is acceptable. Sanctify and mature us in the truth, and help us to grow both in our depth of relationships as well as breadth of understanding. For the sake of Your name, Jesus, Amen.

Chapter 3

HARMONY: A FRESH LOOK AT 1 CORINTHIANS 12

IF unity in the Church was supposed to be easy, a body with different parts wouldn't have been the New Testament analogy of choice—Legos, maybe, where each building block looks similar and is easily interchangeable. Even a color wheel is easier to deal with than a human body; there might be differing opinions on which colors look good together, but at least you're dealing with items from the same category. In a body, it's challenging to notice much similarity between a kneecap and an eardrum, an eyeball and a liver, or a nostril and a femur. All of them are vital, and all of them do indeed work together under the direction of the common head, but each one of them is highly specialized. The human body is as much of a miracle as is the Church when it's functioning like God intended.

Psalm 133 is often the go-to passage in the Old Testament for unity: "How sweet it is when brothers dwell together in unity..." I've done various read-through-the-Bible-in-a-year programs over the last several decades, and while I like to switch up the programs (chronological, different categories of readings each day, etc.), I also like to switch the translations. It's too easy for my mind to move on to the tasks for the day if what I'm reading is overly familiar.

The last couple of years I intentionally chose a more literal translation, the New American Standard. So this year I selected the New Living Translation (NLT) for something completely different. Doing so resulted in a revolutionary surprise, partly because of my present context for ministry. The concept was there the last time I used the NLT, but I missed it. Psalm 133 in the New Living Translation doesn't use the word "unity;" instead, it uses "harmony."

THE LOCAL CONGREGATION DOESN'T HAVE ALL THE PARTS, ISN'T SUPPOSED TO HAVE ALL THE PARTS, AND WILL DIE TRYING TO ATTAIN EVERY PART.

> How wonderful and pleasant it is when brothers live together in harmony! ²For harmony is as precious as the anointing oil that was poured over Aaron's head, that ran down his beard and onto the border of his robe. ³Harmony is as refreshing as the dew from Mount Hermon that falls on the mountains of Zion. And there the Lord has pronounced his blessing, even life everlasting. (Psalm 133: 1–3 NLT)

I live in a household of musicians, and harmony provides a vividly full word picture when it comes to the heart of Jesus' John 17 prayer. Unison singing requires everyone to be on the same note, but harmony is what creates the rich sounds and overtones. When a song has been filled with creative harmony, a unison passage stands out powerfully; but unison all the time is much less engaging. Cameron Hood, the worship leader at our home congregation and a phenomenal, creative musician who is also in the touring band Ryanhood (as well as the graphic designer and typesetter for this book), pointed out that harmony isn't just different notes; it's the rhythm and accompaniment that undergirds the melody. When switching from *a cappella* choral to instrumental music, the picture becomes even closer to the New Testament image of unity. Not only are the instruments playing different notes, the instruments themselves are widely varied: woodwinds, strings, percussion, and brass. They don't look the same, sound the same, operate the same, or carry out the same roles. That's why musical creativity is endless and why Martin Luther once said, "Next to the Word of God, the noble art of music is the greatest treasure in the world."

Unity and uniformity couldn't be further apart. The first time the topic of unity surfaces in John 17, Jesus prays that all believers in Him "may be one as we are one." (John 17:11) It's hard to imagine two beings more different than a Heavenly Father who is omniscient, omnipresent, and omnipotent, and an earthly pray-er who is limited (for the moment) in time, knowledge, location, and power. Right out of the gate, Jesus is praying for the harder road, the narrow road, the road less traveled. Uniformity was easier to achieve, but hardly worthy of Jesus' prayer attention.

A SOLUTION FOR PASTORAL BURNOUT

Speaking of things being easy (or not), if being a pastor was easy, there wouldn't be so many who struggle with depression or quit every month.[1] Could it be that a major part of the reason for pastoral burnout is an inappropriate view of the congregation in the first place? When you ask most people what church they go to, they automatically think of the local congregation. And when most people read through Paul's analogy of the church as a body, most fully developed in 1 Corinthians 12, the most common application is the local congregation. But the starting point when you think church in the New Testament isn't the local congregation, but the citywide Church. How life giving it is to understand that my job as a pastor isn't to shore up every weakness in my

---

1   The most commonly cited number is 1,500–1,700 pastors leave the ministry every month, and 70 percent battle depression regularly. An October 15, 2015 article in *Christianity Today* entitled "That Stat that Says Pastors are All Miserable and Want to Quit (Part 1)" challenged that statistic. While the numbers may be debatable, pastoral burnout is inarguably a very real and common issue, and one with which I personally have struggled.

congregation. How freeing to realize that it was *Jesus' idea* that each congregation is one part of the body, with inherent strengths and weaknesses that no amount of effort, training, or prayer will ever completely eliminate. How enjoyable to set out on a different mission—to discover what God is uniquely calling my congregation to be and become at this point in time rather than trying to be everything to everyone![2]

Whether you're a pastor, a congregational leader, a congregational attendee, or someone burned out on trying to find the perfect church, here is the gospel truth: the local congregation doesn't have all the parts, isn't supposed to have all the parts, and will die trying to attain every part. The congregation isn't the City Church—and it isn't even supposed to be. Play your instrument in the orchestra, sing your part in the choir, and develop harmony with brothers and sisters in the rest of your city.

UNITY TRENDING

Does unity become easy or easier over time? The more time a group spends together, the closer a group gets, right? We know this doesn't hold true in all circumstances, but shouldn't we expect it to hold true if we're talking about Christ followers?

Those in a group who value unity from the outset might more conscientiously submit to one another, or voluntarily hold back on things that could produce conflict, especially at the beginning. Similarly, a couple who is dating each put their best foot forward at the beginning of the relationship. We value the courtship, so we exercise enough self-control to stifle opinions or actions that might create conflict. But over time, the parts of our personalities, gifts, and training that we initially suppress start to manifest themselves. Some of this is good, necessary, and unavoidable, the natural developmental process of a relationship. Psychologist Bruce Tuckman first articulated the memorable phrase "forming, storming, norming, and performing" in his 1965 article, "Developmental Sequence in Small Groups." As you might

---

2   See *Church Unique*, by Will Mancini, for a book written on that very topic.

guess from the terminology, "storming" is where the differences start to surface.

The process of letting our strengths grow, develop, and mature is a thoroughly desirable endeavor, but it will produce conflict. Just like Proverbs 27:17 tells us that "iron sharpens iron" (and probably produces sparks in the process), strength rubbing up against strength will produce some new challenges. As the saying goes, "new levels equal new devils." When various members of a group develop more fully into their God-created strengths and purposes, the challenges of moving from uniformity to harmony increase significantly.

> **DIVERSITY DOESN'T MEAN DIVISION; IT'S BY DESIGN.**

What makes a human body so beautiful and so powerful is the wide variety of its parts. Diversity doesn't mean division; it's by design. *This* is what Jesus was praying for—and what will catch the attention of a watching world. Peter Poppleton said, "Often we settle for a least common denominator unity, where we have to leave behind who we really are in order to enter in." And at the same Good Cities Conference[3] in January 2015, Gary Kinnaman (pastor and leader of the John 17 Movement in Phoenix, AZ) said, "God throws us into the melting pot of differences because we're good for the pot and the pot is good for us." As we've already seen, maturity is an outgrowth of unity.

The section of 1 Corinthians where the "body" analogy gets fully developed is part of a three-chapter discussion on spiritual gifts. The gifts of the Spirit are for the edifying of the body and are intended to grow in strength as they're exercised. How tragic that the gifts of the Spirit themselves have become one of the greatest sources of division within Christianity. Some parts preach against their use, even going so far as to claim that modern day usage of some of the gifts is demonic, while other parts celebrate and highlight the gifts, going so far as to teach that some of the gifts are necessary evidence of salvation.

---

3   Good Cities Conferences are led by Glenn Barth.

That specific challenge was one of the reasons it took until 2009 for Tucson to have its first Pastor Prayer Summit. Evangelical and charismatic pastors weren't even sure they could pray together without the sparks turning into a blaze. Yet through mutual submission to one head, the same group that went up the mountain apprehensive strangers came down as optimistic friends, a visible answer to Jesus' John 17 prayer. The gifts of the Spirit are only one aspect of the Spirit's work; the fruit of the Spirit is just as important. If it was easy, Jesus wouldn't have prayed for it. Unless our character develops as completely as our resume, the stronger we become, the more fractured we're likely to get.

THE DAY EUDY'S AND SYNDY'S EYES OPENED WIDE

That would be Euodia and Syntyche. Okay, be honest now—have you ever even heard of these two women? My wife Valerie is a music specialist in a public elementary school, meaning that she sees 750 kids a week. One year she had to alternate between two schools, bringing the number of her students to 1,500. How many children named Euodia and Syntyche do you suppose she had in class? None is a good (and correct) guess.

The only place you're likely to meet Euodia and Syntyche is in Philippians 4:2–3. Pastor Chris DeHaan of Vineyard Christian Community in Tucson preached a sermon in June 2015 called, "Everyday Unity," and not only did the title immediately grab my attention, but the message was typically awesome. Most of this section is drawn from Chris's sermon.

Unity is a very common theme for the Apostle Paul. In these two short little verses, Paul calls these two women out, and urges a) that the two of them unite, and b) that others in the body help them unite. When Paul's letters were written and delivered, the community gathered together and heard them all at the same time as they were read aloud. Often, the letters were then passed along to the next gathering of believers in the city. Imagine your surprise if you're Eudy or Syndy and three quarters of the way through the letter, you're mentioned by name.

We don't know the nature of their conflict, but we do know that these were faithful, dedicated, godly women. We can't write the conflict off as simply one or two misguided, conflict-seeking individuals. The way Paul talks about them eliminates that option. The first huge takeaway, then, is that conflict is totally normal. A John 17 group of people isn't a group that never has differences; in fact, the only way conflict is completely avoided is if nothing of substance is being undertaken— that nobody cares enough about each other or the mission to disagree.

The solution to the conflict is the second huge takeaway from verse 2 of this passage: "Be of the same mind in the Lord." That command takes a radical 90 degree turn when the phrase "in the Lord" appears. Far from Paul telling them to simply think alike, Paul knows that different parts of the body are bound to think differently—not because of sin, but by design. The command is for both to take on the mind of Christ, which he had already described earlier in the letter in Philippians 2. In following Christ, we die to ourselves, put others first, humble ourselves, and never think more highly of ourselves or our opinions than we should.

The world doesn't need to see a room full of clones marching in lockstep with each other. Leave that to *Star Wars*. The world needs to observe very different people dancing together because of their common love in Christ.

WHEN JESUS IS ALL WE HAVE IN COMMON

For more than a decade, I called my new member classes at the church I served "Christian Appetizers." I extended invitations to people who had visited the congregation, never entirely sure until the first day who was going to attend. At the first meeting, I asked each attendee to share a bit of their personal faith story, regardless of how developed or undeveloped it was, and prayed for God to begin the process of knitting us together into a true Christian community. I also asked the attendees what questions they most wanted to talk about, saying everything was fair game and believing that if the group set the agenda, the buy-in and investment was going to be stronger. By the end of our five-six week journey, the choice of the title "Christian Appetizers" became apparent—this is just the beginning of growing in love for God and for one another; we had the rest of our lives on this Earth to continue growing in both directions.

I formed these groups several times a year, but one still stands out in my memory. My favorite and most memorable group had two of the most different-from-one-another people imaginable. One, named "Sally," was a former topless dancer in her twenties who had struggled through life

> UNLESS OUR CHARACTER DEVELOPS AS COMPLETELY AS OUR RESUME, THE STRONGER WE BECOME, THE MORE FRACTURED WE'RE LIKELY TO GET.

at virtually every level. The consistent grace-filled love of a mature woman old enough to be her grandmother had encouraged "Sally" to give God and the Christian community another try. When she told her story, leaving out very few of the more edgy details, the guy sitting next to her nearly had a heart attack. That was "John," a proper, retired English professor from Oxford whose wife had recently died. He and his wife were recluses with no kids. When she became terminally ill, a niece and nephew came to Tucson, knocked on the door of our church building, explained the situation, and asked us to reach out to our secluded neighbors a block or two away. We had developed a relationship because of that request, and so here he was, in his first ever Christian meeting.

I came home to tell my wife about the new group and commented, "Only Jesus could be reason enough for those two people to land in the same room." Both eventually became part of our congregation, with "John" teaching one of the best classes on C.S. Lewis we'd ever experienced and "Sally" helping us to grow in grace.

Another John 17 cameo happened last year on one of the treasured Sundays when I was able to worship in our new home congregation with no responsibilities elsewhere. I was so moved by what happened in the service that day, I came home and wrote up the experience, shared here precisely as I penned it.

I was worried I might have to catch her when she fell out of her chair.

Sitting a couple rows in front of me during Sunday worship was this frail little lady suffering with Parkinson's. Her commitment to being in the house of God whenever humanly (divinely?) possible is quite a testimony for all of us. But as she would shake, nod off, and start to lean perilously, I was envisioning a dramatic rescue as I leapt forward to catch her before she hit the floor.

My imagined heroics normally aren't necessary, however. This particular week was an exception, not because she was struggling more than usual, but because she normally has a companion in worship to watch out for her, help her with her walker, and look after her needs. And this duo, these two women, are a marvelous cameo of beautiful, biblical unity—a John 17 unity as it were.

Her worship companion appears to be a single, Asian woman in her late twenties or early thirties. How these two women met is unknown to me, but my guess is it's another everyday miracle in the body of Christ—two people with nothing in common but Jesus. When Jesus' prayed that his followers' love for one another would catch the attention of the world, He must have had these two in mind.

Watching these two, it takes about five minutes to notice two things—these two women love and care for one another, and these two women would never have crossed paths except for Jesus leading the way. More, Lord! May we notice more of these stories that are all too common in the body of Christ. And may more of the world have the opportunity to witness and partake of this uncommon Love.

LEARNING TO LIVE UNNATURALLY

I recognize and regularly thank God for my truly unique position: getting paid full time to see Jesus' John 17 prayer answered in our city. I didn't have the luxury and blessing as a congregational pastor to build relationships intentionally across so broad and diverse a spectrum of the Body of Christ. Very few people have that privilege. But all of us can do something.

One of the messages I've preached several times around town is called "Love the Other Other." We're all naturally drawn to those with whom we have things in common. Perhaps it's people at the same stage in life, from the same ethnic or cultural background, with similar leisure or entertainment interests, or experiencing the same life challenges. Have you noticed that similar body parts group together in the human body, too? Fingers aren't randomly spread out, eyeballs are parallel and only a few inches from one another, hair is—okay, skip that one. I don't believe there's anything wrong with taking the "low hanging fruit" approach in human relationships, connecting at deep levels without lots of built-in roadblocks.

However, in the Body of Christ, that can't be the whole story. Common love (see Chapter 6 of *Jesus' Surprising Strategy*) must be supplemented by uncommon love with a divine origin and explanation if Jesus' prayer is to be fully answered and the world adequately wowed. We're called to step out of our comfort zones, live *un*naturally, walk across the room, and learn to love the *other* other.[4] Randy Reynolds, founder and director of Community Renewal in Tucson, AZ, regularly points to a map of the city that shows the neighborhoods that are most

---

4   Bill Hybels wrote an incredibly powerful, simple, and applicable book and subsequent series entitled, *Walk Across the Room*.

stressed with factors such as crime and poverty. His constant plea is for the well-resourced congregations (in terms of dollars and leaders) to find ways to walk across the city and connect with congregations that are under-resourced, because both participants and the entire city will benefit if they do.

There are plenty of relationships that make total sense without Jesus having anything to do with them. Let's engage in some that will be impossible without Jesus as the source and glue.

LEARNING FROM THE WORLD OF SPORTS

Why will 50,000 spectators fill a football stadium and 20,000 pack a basketball arena, at high cost in both time and money? Could it be because they're watching sports teams do what God called the Church to do? A body is God's design, implicitly attractive. But sports teams typically operate closer to the Manufacturer's specifications than the City Church does. Specializing is inherently challenging, yet it's second nature for sports teams functioning at the highest level. The teams that are the most enjoyable to watch (and usually the most successful) have learned how to successfully encourage every person to play their part uniquely while each voluntarily submits to one another out of reverence for—for what? The game? Victory? The coach? Whatever or whoever it is, sports teams have learned to specialize to the extreme while simultaneously setting aside personal preferences.

THERE ARE PLENTY OF RELATIONSHIPS THAT MAKE TOTAL SENSE WITHOUT JESUS HAVING ANYTHING TO DO WITH THEM.

One example came from my beloved University of Arizona Wildcat basketball team's Bay Area campus, also known as the Golden State Warriors. After winning the National Basketball Association championship in 2015 and breaking the all-time record for most wins in a regular season the following year, the Warriors made an odd decision:

they traded away some parts to add another superstar (Kevin Durant) to their preexisting collection of superstars.

Some of the comments after the trades were fascinating. "You have to figure out how to blend it all," new teammate Stephen Curry said. "But everybody has to be 100 percent themselves. When it comes to the full culture of our team, it'll take a minute to flow." Ananth Pandian wrote for CBS Sports, "Durant was asked for a fuller explanation on why he picked the Warriors. He called it an 'easy choice.' 'It felt like it was a perfect fit. It was something I was searching for when I sat down and talked to these guys. I wanted to see if what I've heard and what I've seen on the outside is really true. Do these guys really genuinely love each other? They work together. You hear family a lot. That's just a word sometimes, but this is really a lifestyle here. You can feel it when you walk in the door, in the practice facility, everybody is just together. That's something that I can appreciate as a basketball player and someone who values relationships. You can tell that that's what they stand on, that's what we stand on. I feel really grateful to play for a team like that and play with a bunch of players who are selfless and enjoy the game in its purest form.'"

It isn't painful or arduous for me to cite and celebrate quotes from a team full of former Wildcats and well-regarded Christ followers who happen to be on a franchise I followed way back in junior high. Suffering for the Lord in these paragraphs—not! But in an act of true humility on my part, here's a quote from a member of the Dallas Cowboys, a team I've cheered against all my life. Quarterback Tony Romo had never made it to the Super Bowl and was arguably playing on the best team of his career in 2016 when he was injured near the start of the season and replaced by a rookie who performed very well. When it was announced that the rookie was going to keep the starting job despite Romo recovering enough to be able to play, here's what Romo said at a press conference:

> "I can remember when I was a kid just starting out and wanting to be part of something bigger than myself. For

every high school kid or college player out there, there's greatness in being the kind of teammate who truly wants to be part of the team. Everyone wants to be the reason they're winning or losing; every single one of us wants to be *that* person. But there are special moments that come from a shared commitment to play your role, while doing it together. That's what you'll remember—not your stats or the prestige, but the relationships and the achievement you created through a group. It's hard to do, but there's great joy in that. And all the while your desire burns to be the best you've ever been. You *can* be both; I've figured that out in this process. It's what separates sports from everything else. It's why we love it, it's why we trust it, it's why I still want to play and compete. Lastly, I want to leave you with something I've learned in this process as well. I feel like we all have two battles, or two enemies going on. One with the man across from you; the second is with the man inside of you. I think once you control the one inside of you, the one across from you really doesn't matter."

Theologically, I take issue with one thing Romo said: "It's what separates sports from everything else. It's why we love it, it's why we trust it..." That's almost a textbook definition of idolatry—and it is hard to identify a higher-ranked idol in our country than sports. (Full disclosure: guilty as charged; sports idolatry is one of my most significant temptations.) But replace sports with Jesus and His Body-of-Christ-on-Earth in the Romo quote, and you've got the answer to Jesus' prayer in John 17.

LEARNING FROM PARENTING

After about the fifth time someone asked, "Are you watching the new TV series, *This is Us?*" my family decided to dive in. (Spoiler alert: if you're planning on watching the series, skip this section, as I'm about to reveal something significant from the series premiere.) A married Anglo couple is expecting triplets when the mom goes into premature labor, and one of the triplets dies. Simultaneously, an unrelated African-American single dad (the mom is out of the picture) decides to give up his newborn, and the couple adopts this third child as their own. The whole series focuses on the parenting relationships that extend into adulthood, and while the values (especially the sexual ones) of the series certainly aren't all biblical, the family relationships are insightful and carefully developed.

> NO PARENT WANTS THEIR CHILDREN TO PRETEND TO BE LIKE THE REST.

In one poignant scene, the dad of the triplets is talking with the adopted son who's about eight years old. This black son, who is academically more gifted than his adopted siblings, had been hiding his knowledge and pretending to be less intelligent than he was to better fit in. The dad gives a powerful speech about how the goal isn't for all the children to be or become identical, even though their parents love each of them equally.

Any parent of more than one child can relate to the challenge. Parenting techniques that work for one child may not work for the next one. As parents, we want to love all our children equally and avoid favoritism, but that can't mean treating each of them as clones. No parent wants their children to pretend to be like the rest. In fact, the opposite is more often the case; we want them to excel in the unique ways God has created them. If parenting was easy—well, someday that could be another book.

DISSONANCE

If harmony was easy, it wouldn't be so interesting. Dissonance is what happens when harmony is less than pleasing to the ear. Dissonance is conflict that's begging to be resolved.

In Jesus' opening thesis of His famous teaching in the Gospel of Matthew, the entire story of Christian community is laid out step by step in what are commonly referred to as the Beatitudes (Matthew 5:1–12).

The first step is "Blessed are the poor in spirit." Humility is the prerequisite for calling on a Savior, and it's the key to building Christian community as well. Those who recognize their brokenness and will admit their need are those who "mourn," which literally means to show on the outside what's happening on the inside. Continuing through the Beatitudes, when we go down into the waters of brokenness and mourning, we come up "meek," which doesn't mean weak, but rather strength under control. And we also "hunger and thirst for righteousness," wanting others to experience the same joy and healing of salvation that we've experienced. This process creates people who are "merciful," who will deal graciously with others whose need for a Savior is evident. "Pure in heart" doesn't refer to perfection, but rather one who truly wants what Jesus wants since Jesus alone is completely pure in heart. "Peacemakers," as opposed to peacekeepers, are those who won't rest until there's true *shalom*—those who will speak the truth in love and address injustice until it's resolved. These peacemakers can expect to experience "persecution," not all the time, but for certain some of the time.

Not everyone will celebrate true peace. Some benefit from injustice. If people persecuted Jesus, the perfect peacemaker, we can certainly expect that they'll occasionally persecute His followers. He told us as much directly (John 15:20). When persecution, opposition, and testing come, the depth of unity is revealed. "In this world you will have trouble. But take heart! I have overcome the world." (John 16:33)

Sadly, when one part of the Body of Christ is attacked by innuendo and libel, the rest of the Body of Christ often does not behave like a healthy physical body does—rallying to the point of need. Instead of "when one part suffers, all suffer with it," the reality is that when one part suffers, many other parts scatter and run for the hills. We've observed this time and again when faith-unfriendly local media members have taken out unjustifiable hit pieces on Christian groups. What causes some of us to flee? I believe the answer is as simple as one small yet powerful word: fear. Yet the Bible tells us that "perfect love drives out fear." (1 John 4:18) Fear is truly dissonant and at odds with divine love, the prayed-for command of Jesus.

The fire of opposition reveals whether the love binding together the Body of Christ is merely human or of divine origin. God's love, perfect love, love that has its source and depth in God, drives out fear so that "together we stand." When one part of the Body of Christ is maligned and attacked, other parts of the Body of Christ who are filled with divine love rush to the scene of the crime, stand with the harmed member, and make the whole Church stronger as a result. Love that is less than that can be damaged by fear.

The dissonance created by external opposition reveals the depth and ultimate source of the love that binds us together—for better or worse. The dissonance caused by internal opposition reveals the source of authority to which the body parts are appealing.

"If we're connected to the same Head (Jesus), we're in the same body" has become one of my favorite statements. But it isn't the last word to eliminate all squirming. How closely connected to the Head do we need to be? Do we have to have the same definitions of the Head to qualify? "Jesus plus nothing" must be the source and ultimate definition of our unity, but what happens when it sounds like we're talking about a different Jesus? Someone must distinguish between what's integral and indispensable versus what's peripheral and optional, especially when our conversations with the Head ask for opposite things (such as prayers for the sanctity of traditional marriage versus prayers for blessing homosexual marriage, or prayers for abortion to end versus prayers for it to remain legal). "Prayer wars" aren't my idea of a good time.

I don't claim to have all the answers, but I do know that hanging out with very different parts of the same body in the City Church has revealed in powerful ways how incomplete some of my previous answers had been. The truth truly does sanctify and purify our unity. Unity and truth themselves must function like iron sharpening iron, regardless of the volume and intensity of the sparks produced.

Sometimes spending time with different parts of the Body of Christ reveals blind spots for many or all, and the dissonance resolves into pleasing harmony. But that isn't always the case; sometimes more effective listening simply serves to sharpen the conflict, not diminish it. Should all dissonance be resolved; *can* all dissonance be resolved? Another way to frame the same question is, "Do all paths lead to the same destination?" Without getting too philosophical, we know that in the natural, the answer is they do not. Theologically, the question then becomes, "Is there truly only one Head and one body, just different ways of describing that Head and living out that body? Or are there in fact different Heads (gods) altogether?" A commitment to being civil to and respectful of one another, while godly and advisable, is different altogether than a commitment to unify as members of the same body.

Here's how I address that question, particularly if it's posed by someone for whom biblical authority can't be the starting point if the conversation is going to get off the ground. I expect God to be bigger than me. A god whom I could fully understand would be by definition no bigger than I am, and therefore not worthy of my worship or obedience. As an act of faith (though based on plenty of evidence and experience, as well as biblical witness), I trust that God is also good and wants my best. Therefore, I willingly choose to submit to His authority and wisdom; my job isn't to come up with my own answers as much as it is to seek out His. For many reasons beyond the primary purpose of this book, I believe the best place to start in discerning God's will and identity is with Jesus Himself, God incarnate, who chose to enter our world fully and completely in order that we might know Him well. Throughout His entire earthly life, Jesus acknowledged the authoritative function of the Scriptures in discerning truth from error. As His follower, it only makes sense for me to do the same. By faith, then, I accept the Bible as the foundational platform, the normative authority for matters of faith and life, and a primary way I show my faith and trust in God.

When considering if all dissonance should or can be resolved, we must understand that when the parties are expressing viewpoints or priorities that appear to conflict, unity and truth must be called upon to dance together, not annihilate the other. Mutual, humble conversation can reveal whether one or both has blind spots that are coming to light with maturity and growth as the result, or if there is in fact a fundamental disagreement. If both parties are appealing to the same authority (the Bible) yet arriving at different conclusions, then either more conversation is needed or a mutual submission out of reverence for Christ is required where we agree to disagree because the fundamentals are held in common and we're clearly worshiping and serving the same Lord. That kind of disagreement/dissonance adds texture and life to the Christian journey and highlights the content of Jesus' prayer—love for every other part of the Body of Christ, not agreement and uniformity in everything.

However, sometimes it may have appeared at first that both parties were singing off of the same sheet of music, but as more conversation takes place, it becomes clear that both aren't appealing to the same ultimate authority at all. Our starting place, then, is to stand under the truth of the Bible. I believe there's plenty of room for dissonance in our Christian song when all parties are working off the same musical score. But Jesus and the Scriptures that reveal Him both draw some lines in the sand. When it becomes clear that one party is appealing to some other higher authority—like their personal experience, perspective on human reason, or some other writing held in higher regard than the Bible—then we are no longer functioning as members of the same body submitting to the same Head, but different bodies altogether. That dissonance should be acknowledged rather than proclaiming "peace, peace" where there is no peace (Jeremiah 6:14).

JESUS AND THE SCRIPTURES THAT REVEAL HIM BOTH DRAW SOME LINES IN THE SAND.

If you're finding unity to be pretty easy, you probably need to get out more. If your congregation or small group never experiences conflict or dissonance, I must ask three hard questions: 1) Are you taking Jesus' commands seriously and really going for it in your mission to be His followers together? 2) Have you limited membership in your group to those who you'd probably love well even without Jesus? 3) Are you keeping everything at a surface level rather than truly being real with one another?

Don't settle for uniformity when harmony is what the Bible describes as precious and refreshing. If your group or congregation is truly homogenous, then start building some relationships (either on your own or as a group) with another homogenous group that looks nothing like yours in age, ethnicity, denominational background, or passion. Any song that drives Jesus to His knees to labor over in prayer *has* to be worth the price of admission.

Few facets of our country better illustrate the vital need for the concepts expressed thus far to be put into practice than the arenas of race relationships and politics. That's where we turn next.

QUESTIONS FOR SELF-REFLECTION

- What analogy speaks most to you about the unity Jesus prayed for—a human body, musical harmony, team sports, parenting, or one of your own? What insights do you gain?

- How does your view of a congregation change when understanding that the congregation is only one part of the City Church? As a pastor? As a member? As a visitor?

- What has been your experience with this statement—"Unless our character develops as completely as our resume, the stronger we become, the more fractured we're likely to get"—with family members, and with brothers and sisters in Christ?

- In the discussion on dissonance, what do you find most challenging in keeping unity and truth together rather than picking one over the other?

TODAY'S GPS

Almighty Creator, Heavenly Father, we praise You for making the world with such astonishing diversity and creativity. Thank You that creation itself testifies to Your power and goodness, and that both inside and outside the Church we can witness the beauty of multiple dissimilar pieces uniting to create stunning displays. We glorify You, Jesus, for taking on flesh and entering this challenging world where sparks fly, the worst of which You allowed to land directly on You. That You would choose to endure persecution on our behalf is humbling beyond words. Protect us from the enemy who would instill fear when persecution strikes parts of the body. What the enemy meant for evil, use for good by leading us to bond together even more closely. Finally, sanctify us in Your truth so that we truly can discern essential and multi-faceted truth from deal-breaking error. May our dissonance resolve into pleasing harmony that leads the world to come to know You, the Songwriter. Amen.

Chapter Four

CROSS CULTURE: THE PATH TO RACIAL RECONCILIATION

IF it was easy to bridge the racial divides in our country, wouldn't we have done it already? Wouldn't the civil rights movement have largely solved it? Wouldn't the election of our first non-Anglo president in 2008 have sealed it—or at least accelerated the progress? Yet as a nation in recent years, we've clearly regressed, not progressed.

If "easy" was the goal, I wouldn't touch this chapter.

If I've learned anything in the last six years, it's how easy it is to misunderstand and be misunderstood. And since 90 percent of communication is non-verbal, I'm at a 90 percent disadvantage right out of the gate. The content of this chapter should be shared in a discussion over coffee. More specifically, it belongs in the context of deeply committed relationships developed over significant amounts of time (the topic of the next chapter) because racial reconciliation is an indispensable piece of unity/harmony in the Body of Christ—and it starts with developing a "Cross culture."

What do I mean by that? As Christians, any discussion of reconciliation, racial or otherwise, starts with the cross. When Jesus is lifted up, He draws all people to Himself (John 12:32). As people of the cross, we therefore have a unique starting point—Christ Himself—to help personally experience racial reconciliation. We do not start with ourselves, our skin colors, our histories, or our differences, but with the cross that binds us all together. This is a point that Mike Alameda, director of Corazón Ministries in Tucson who does cross cultural training, makes regularly. This reality will be primarily identified from here forward as "Cross culture," with "cross" capitalized to remove any confusion with the already universally recognized term "cross culture," which may or may not have anything to do with Jesus' cross.

> WE DO NOT START WITH OURSELVES, OUR SKIN COLORS, OUR HISTORIES, OR OUR DIFFERENCES, BUT WITH THE CROSS THAT BINDS US ALL TOGETHER.

My friend, colleague, and mentor Pastor Paul Anderson uses a "broken toe" analogy born out of personal experience. When he broke his toe several years ago, he was surprised at how protective of it he was afterward. He'd walk a wide berth around every piece of furniture and instinctively stick his arms out around people to keep them from accidentally stepping on the injured appendage. I mention this because race remains a raw topic in our country, with ongoing incidents that irritate the wound and exacerbate the tension. Caution and tentativeness are therefore wise, for the soothing balm of grace is the only environment in which healing and reconciliation are possible.

THE NEED FOR CROSS CULTURE: SOUTH CAROLINA TRAGEDY

Since the power of story will be one of the suggestions at the end of the chapter, I'll start with one of my own—one that introduces us to the Cross culture being lived out in the midst of unspeakable tragedy—but not by everyone. This is based on a blog I wrote on June 24, 2015, entitled "South Carolina Wake-Up Call."

> The horrific murder of nine people at Emanuel African Methodist Episcopal Church in Charleston, South Carolina one week ago was a powerful wake up call for me. But not in the ways you might guess.

> As a quick recap, a 21-year-old Anglo male came into the church last Wednesday night, sat through the hour-long Bible study and prayer meeting, and then murdered nine people, intentionally leaving one woman alive so that she could tell the world his reasons for the killing. He killed them because they were black. He later said that they were so nice to him he almost didn't kill them. Wow. While the "niceness" of these Christians wasn't enough to save their lives, his racial hatred also wasn't enough to stop their Christ-like behavior. Their response has been absolutely patterned after Jesus Christ, as they have made public statements of forgiveness and love to him repeatedly and consistently. That's the Cross culture personified.

> When I first became the Church Domain Director for 4Tucson, one of the very first imperatives that God gave me was to build bridges to the African-American and Hispanic churches and pastors in Tucson. It's not citywide unity in the body of Christ if it's predominantly Anglo. The relationships I've built with these dear brothers and sisters in Christ over the last four years have become one of the richest blessings of my life. This aspect of my "work" isn't "work" at all—it's sheer blessing. I've become so aware of my ignorance in so many arenas, and am very grateful for all of the blind spots that I had that God has now revealed to me. Blind spots are by definition negative; therefore,

the removal of them is essential and entirely positive. I just had no idea how far I have to go.

I read some articles about the tragedy last Thursday morning. "How horrible," I thought. And then I moved on with my day. I was the Master of Ceremonies for our monthly Tucson Ministry Alliance meeting that happened over lunch on Thursday, and I was focused on all of the great things that God is doing in opening up doors for Christians to be salt and light in our public schools. They really *are* great things—worthy of tremendous celebration. Everyone who came was genuinely blessed. There were fewer African-Americans there that day than normal in hindsight, but I didn't notice it at the time. Not once did it cross my mind to have a moment of prayer for our grieving brothers and sisters in South Carolina. Not once did I lament that racism is still alive and well in our country, much more alive than nine victims from a sister church. And not once did any of the guests there—probably 80 or so—mention it either. None of us thought about publicly acknowledging this tragedy, or if some did think about it, nobody took the initiative to say so.

I'd love to tell you that once my mind was less focused on my responsibilities, I realized immediately the missed opportunity. But I didn't. I didn't think about it the rest of the day. This tragedy had been neatly compartmentalized into a very small box. The light didn't dawn until the next morning when a dear friend who had led prayer at the meeting contacted me and confessed his sorrow and shock that he hadn't thought about including this the day before. How could I have forgotten something that I profess to deeply care about? Regardless of race, how could I have not been more affected by a tragedy that ought to have struck closer to home? How many Wednesday night Bible studies did I lead at my church over 20-plus years? Probably nearly 1,000. The racial component to the tragedy should have *significantly added* to its impact on me. My friend put it best—"I'm shocked at how much I take racial reconciliation for granted."

Did any of my black friends forget to mention this at any of their meetings on Thursday? I doubt it. The New Testament picture of the Body of Christ is that when one part suffers, all suffer together. For all our advancements as a country since the 1960s in aspects of racial unity, we have a really, really long way to go when not only does someone raised in our country come out so gripped by evil and blind hatred as this young man, but when it's primarily our African-American communities nationally that are deeply moved by this tragedy.

WHEN WILL REAL PROGRESS BE EVIDENT? WHEN WHITE COMMUNITIES ARE AS GRIEVED BY RACISM AS NON-WHITE COMMUNITIES ARE.

When will real progress be evident? When white communities are as grieved by racism as non-white communities are.

I have two things to confess— I'm not as compassionate as I'd like to be . . . and as Jesus is. And apparently, I'm not as connected to the rest of the body as I'd like to be . . . and thought I was. That's the story of Cross culture missing in action.

"If one part suffers, every part suffers with it; if one part is honored, every part rejoices with it." (1 Corinthians 12:26) That's a definitive distinctive of the Cross culture—but it sadly hasn't been characterized as often as it should in the Body of Christ, especially when we're talking about ethnic parts of the body. Our isolation has denied us the reconciling power of the cross in places where it's desperately needed.

To my white friends, here's a sneak peek on where this is going to encourage you to resist the temptation to skip over this chapter: "The answer to white privilege is not white guilt." If the phrase "white privilege" is confusing or makes you bristle (both reactions were part of my very recent history), guilt over our skin color is not the suggested solution. Jesus is the good news of the gospel; His prayer reflects the good news of the gospel, and I've run this past several other people before publishing it to ensure that in the end, "good news" is its final flavor.

To my other-than-white friends, read what's to come as if you were an elementary school teacher reading a fourth-grade essay. You've taught me a lot, but I'm sure I'm revealing as much of my ignorance as I am what I've already learned. Help me keep learning. Thank you, so many of you, for helping even with this chapter.

My final caveat is that this is a chapter in a book, not an entire book. I haven't learned enough to write a whole book on this topic; there are plenty of others who have. I'll reference some of them throughout the chapter. For the scope of this book, I'm limiting the perspective to lessons learned about the Cross culture being applied to racial reconciliation in the context of seeking to see Jesus' prayer for unity/harmony answered in my own city.

CLASH OF CULTURES

Race and ethnicity bring with them cultures, and the clash of cultures is often the root of the issue rather than racism, per se. From Dr. Tom Wisley, an international expert on cross cultural training and a good friend:

> "Racism" is simply politicized ethnocentrism. Ethnocentrism is essentially the view that "my culture is better than yours" and your culture/race is inferior to mine.

The reason we need to define the term is that to deal with racism responsibly, we need to know what it is. What we end up doing is treating "racism" as a political issue rather than a cultural one; hence, we don't take proper steps to deal with it. Workshops on "What is Culture?" or "Cultural Worldviews" could bring understanding and tolerance, while treating it as a political issue often brings intolerance, anger, and judgmentalism.

As followers of Christ, we seek a Cross culture—not the culture of our skin color. Our primary identity is as a Christ follower, not whatever ethnic box the government forms ask us to check. Each of those ethnic cultures are gifts from a gracious Giver, and under the cross, they can join together to create the harmony the world so desperately seeks to see, hear, and experience. Under the cross, we can make room for plenty of diversity because diversity doesn't imply division; it is by design.

MY FIRST CROSS CULTURE INSIGHT

On August 9, 2014, an 18-year-old African-American male named Michael Brown was shot and killed by an Anglo police officer, Darren Wilson, in Ferguson, MO. A jury eventually heard the case, but in the meantime, it was tried in the court of public opinion. Protests spilled out into the streets, not only in St. Louis but around the country.

Because our Pastors Partnership of primarily African-American and Anglo pastors had been meeting monthly for nearly two years at that time, we had created a built-in, Cross culture place where we could come together and say, "Help me understand your perspective." We had established through previous conversation and prayer that our unity in Christ was sufficient to enable us to address and talk through our differences rather than ignore them. The next week, one of the African-American pastors, Grady Scott, joined me on our daily radio program, 4Tucson at 4, to discuss what we were learning. Pastor Scott asked us Anglos, "What's the first question you asked when you heard about the Michael Brown shooting?" Nearly unanimously, we answered,

"What were the details of the situation?" Pastor Scott said, "The first thing we African-Americans asked was, 'How does this connect to other similar situations?'"

Many non-Anglo cultures are more group oriented or "communal," emphasizing the extended family or village/tribal members, while Anglo cultures tend to emphasize the individual.[1] We start from different places, we evaluate circumstances differently, and we view the world through different lenses. With all the various incidents of white police officers shooting black men, the first question that innately crosses my mind is, "What were the circumstances in each case?" But others' first question is, "Is there a connection? Is there something systemic going on?"

Is one question better than the other? Is one cultural perspective or lens more accurate or helpful than the other? No and No. We need both perspectives. As Pastor and Director of Morningstar Ministries Rick Joyner

WHEN PUTTING A PUZZLE TOGETHER, DO YOU NEED ALL THE PIECES OR THE WHOLE PICTURE? BOTH, OF COURSE!

says, "It takes two wings to fly." In the Ferguson shooting, the judicial system needed to weigh the evidence of the case at hand; we want to be tried on the basis of our own situation, not somebody else's. But we also recognize that we always bring our biases with us, and systems can become biased just as easily as individuals can, so we need to ask the bigger questions, too. Tucson Pastor Elwood McDowell, part of our Pastors Partnership, points out that many of the other recent incidences of police violence appear to have a stronger racial component than the Ferguson shooting because he said the Brown case "too easily lets a white reader feel like the whole problem is exaggerated by black people." That fear reveals the extent of our brokenness, pointing us once again to the cross where in Christ the dividing walls of hostility are broken down.

---

1   See Charles H. Kraft, *Anthropology For Christian Witness*, pgs. 150–160.

When putting a puzzle together, do you need all the pieces or the whole picture? Both, of course! Racism isn't just an individual experience (the way I used to think about it); there are also systemic issues that can't be seen if individual stories are isolated from one another and never seen as a whole. The single most helpful thing I've learned on this topic is that when "racism" is mentioned, we probably aren't even talking about the same thing, i.e. individual versus systemic. To illustrate, a 2016 Barna Research study revealed that 84 percent of all Americans see racial tension as a significant issue in our country, crossing every demographic sector. Yet Evangelicals are twice as likely as any other group to see racism as primarily a problem of the past.[2]

Finally, sociology and communication theory have taught us that complete neutrality is a myth; we are always going to view the world through our cultural and experiential lenses. Those lenses aren't just individual but collective—to the point that the news channel a person identifies with most closely is a strong indicator of the political party they lean toward. Does the media have a bias? Of course it does. Does that bias affect how the "facts" of cases such as those already mentioned are discussed? Certainly. The answer? A Cross culture experience where we live not for ourselves, but for others.

RACE, POLITICS, AND THE CHURCH

Apostle Warren Anderson, the founder of our Pastors Partnership group, says, "At the core in politics you'll always find the issue of race." I'm sure he's not alone in that viewpoint; he's just the first person I've heard articulate it so succinctly.

Our country is more divided politically than perhaps at any time in our nation's history. A June 12, 2014 article from the Pew Research Center entitled "Political Polarization in the American Public: How Increasing Ideological Uniformity and Partisan Antipathy Affect Politics, Compromise and Everyday Life" shows the dramatically growing division just from the

---

2   Barna, "Black Lives Matter and Racial Tension in America", Research Releases in Culture and Media, May 5, 2016.

last 20 years—but most of us probably don't need research to know the division is increasing. I've started intentionally viewing dueling news media outlets simultaneously, one supportive of the left and one supportive of the right, in the hopes that I can discern what's really happening somewhere in between. My wife has done the same thing, and she recently heard a commentator on National Public Radio aptly say, "We get our news from echo chambers which merely repeat what we already believe."

Of all the demographic factors—geography, gender, economics, race, and education—that determine which political party a person is likely to support or join, the strongest seems to be race.[3] Our nation's racial divide is significantly fueling our political divide. The political divide is so wide that we're experiencing the exact opposite of what the Bible teaches in 1 Corinthians 12:26: when one political part of our country suffers, the rest rejoice, and vice versa. Framed positively, if the Church will take the lead in improving race relationships, which is possible as the cross of Jesus is lifted high, the Body of Christ could significantly help our country heal politically. If conversations on racial reconciliation become common in the Body of Christ, everyone wins. As Christ followers, we should never again have to choose in an election between which vulnerable population to protect: the unborn or the immigrant. We shouldn't have to choose between which biblical value to champion: the sanctity of marriage or care for the poor. Only our brokenness and division forces us into those kinds of choices. Cross culture, personified in us, can take both us and our country to healthier, more whole places.

Quoting Apostle Anderson on another aspect of the conversation, he says, "Racism is a spirit—who else but the Church can address it? The Church has been given the ministry of reconciliation." Citing an example from his hometown, he adds, "The churches in Chicago still can't unite enough to bring Heaven to Earth and quench the spirit of murder." Could the nation's problems point in part to our isolation as Christ followers and corresponding immaturity? "You are the salt of the earth . . . You are the light of the world" from Matthew 5:13–14 aren't commands, but declarations. The religious community in Jesus' day

---

3   See *Beyond Racial Gridlock*, by George Yancey, for one of the best discussions on these issues.

was compared to leaven flowing through and affecting the entire loaf, and the comparison wasn't a positive one: "Be on your guard against the yeast of the Pharisees and Sadducees." (Matthew 16:6) Have we sown immaturity into the culture by our lack of unity/harmony in the Body of Christ?

One way to appreciate the magnitude of our country's division was a cursory perusal of my Facebook feed after the grand jury's decision over the Ferguson shooting was announced. One said, "It doesn't take 100 days to figure out if murder is a crime; it takes 100 days to figure out how to say it isn't," while another said, "The reaction is so ridiculous they ought to let the whole place burn." And those were the fit-for-print reactions.

It takes something bigger than the gap to bridge the gap. Common faith in Jesus Christ is the only thing I know that's

OUR COUNTRY IS MORE DIVIDED POLITICALLY THAN PERHAPS AT ANY TIME IN OUR NATION'S HISTORY.

bigger than the cultural and political gap between races. That isn't just a theoretical statement; it's born from experience over the past six years working for John 17 unity/harmony. For example, when city-wide Christian gatherings equally represented by Latinos and Anglos addressed the topic of immigration, one of the comments I heard multiple times was, "This is the first time I've really been able to hear and appreciate the other side of the argument." Cross culture was being experienced both culturally and theologically.

I had the opportunity to preach in my home congregation the Sunday after the November 2016 elections, and I got permission from the leadership to address politics in the message. I called it "Anti-Compartmentalization," part of a series called "Jesus Goes Out," and here's what I shared:

> Compartmentalizing spills over into our lack of unity; we stay in our own compartments ethnically and

denominationally. Jesus thought this was a really serious problem, according to John 17. As a result, there's a lack of maturity because we keep all of our blind spots. I've seen in print and heard from people's mouths several times this last week, "You can't be a Christian and vote for a Democrat," or, "You have to be racist if you're voting Republican." It would be one thing if that's what the world was saying, but those statements are from Christ followers! The only way those words get said is if we've never actually sat down and talked and prayed and worshiped and built relationships with the folks we're talking about—because we don't demonize our friends. Jesus went out! We have to go out, walk across the room, develop relationships with other Christ followers who see things differently, and say, "Help me understand your perspective" rather than "Here's why you should adopt mine." If we do that, the salt and light we'll influence our culture with is maturity instead of immaturity. Jesus' John 17 prayer for unity might actually be our country's best, if not only, hope, too. Jesus came to break down the dividing walls of hostility—all of them.

At least in Tucson, the racial and cultural challenges within the Christian community aren't so much animosity as isolation. You don't have to be racist—believing your race is superior to others—to live in an ethnic silo with little to no interaction with other ethnic or cultural parts of the Body of Christ. But if isolation isn't dealt with, not only will problems and challenges in our city and in ourselves go unaddressed; the greater tragedy is all the blessings that will go unexperienced.

I mentioned in Chapter 3 that the statement from Proverbs 27:17 that "iron sharpens iron" implies sparks. I believe that we're suffering from iron deficiency in the Body of Christ—and our society is paying the price. At our 4Tucson staff meeting a week after the presidential election, Chief Operating Officer and Vice President of the Domains and Taskforces Division Tony Simms asked all of us to share what Proverbs 27:17 meant to them. One person, Karen Henley, had a grandfather who was a blacksmith. She described "iron sharpening iron" as a brutal process that requires heating up the metal until it's malleable. The day before when our Pastors Partnership group met, there were some sparks. Yet with a common Lord and over four years of relational equity established, when the conversation heated up, some listening, changing, and shaping resulted. The meeting ended with a call and commitment to spend every day we met together in prayer and fasting. That's the Cross culture experience at its best.

Or how about this? January 20, 2017, the day of President Trump's inauguration, our Pastors Partnership shared an evening of great food, worship, praise, and prayer *together* in the home of one of the African-American pastors. Mutual vulnerability graced the evening, and there wasn't a hint of division despite the different perspectives present. Cross culture tasted even better than the meal we shared to start the evening.

Does the world care what the Church does about race relationships? Yes! *Arizona Daily Star* reporter Johanna Willett attended a Religious News Association conference, and she sat in on a panel in which the comment was made that black and white pastors rarely connect with one another for the purpose of racial reconciliation. "It's happening in Tucson," she thought, and came back to write an article about it, published October 23, 2016. I received numerous positive comments on Facebook from my non-churched friends. More than six weeks later, I was playing racquetball with some gym rats at the YMCA when one of them brought up the article and wanted to hear more about what we were doing, leading to a conversation that continued weeks later.

After the South Carolina shootings, our Pastors Partnership group sponsored a citywide worship service called "Love Conquers Hate," where we took time to read the quotations from family members who pronounced forgiveness and love in the face of such stark hatred that had personally robbed them. The community response was phenomenal. Two city council members attended, resulting in multiple conversations in subsequent weeks where city government officials reached out to the Church for help and answers. In 2016, after a rash of police shootings nationwide and growing tension, we held another worship service called "Love Conquers Racism," and again it was clear that both the Church and the community are hungry for the love for which Jesus prayed in John 17.

"THE MOST SEGREGATED HOUR"

As you read this next section, please keep in mind my opening comments about misunderstanding at the start of the chapter as I pray that this section will generate some meaningful reflection regardless of whether everyone shares its conclusion.

In 1960, Rev. Dr. Martin Luther King Jr. referred to 11:00 Sunday morning as "the most segregated hour in America." Racial segregation was enforced in many parts of the country at the time Dr. King made this statement, yet it seems that I hear that quote quite often today, long after racial segregation was deemed illegal. While there are likely a higher number of congregations who are more racially diverse than in 1960, it's safe to say that most congregations today are still predominantly one race. Should all congregations be racially diverse—or at least as racially diverse as the neighborhood in which they worship?

In groups where racial reconciliation is a stated goal, the assumed answer to that question is usually "yes." While I'm not prepared to go as far as to say "no," I do wish to pose an alternative possibility based on the previous chapter about harmony. If we understand the Church to be the entire Christian Church in the city, not just a local congregation, then each local congregation is and always will be only one part of the Body of Christ. The goal isn't to get every part to look the same, with every congregation blending its music, activities,

> HAVE WE SOWN IMMATURITY INTO THE CULTURE BY OUR LACK OF UNITY/HARMONY IN THE BODY OF CHRIST?

worship, and ethnicity in equal proportions. Besides being an unachievable goal, in my opinion it's also an undesirable goal.

Worship in particular is a matter of the heart, not a series of motions. Pastor Angel Morfin, a dear Hispanic friend and brother who is also the Associate Church Domain Director with 4Tucson, is both bilingual and bicultural, but when he prays, he prefers to pray in Spanish because it's his "heart language." When I attend Latino services, even if translation is provided, it's still harder to get into the flow of the service because I can't appreciate the beauty and flow of the foreign language. Literal languages aren't the only "languages" involved, either: there's formality versus informality, structure as opposed to spontaneity, quiet reverence versus raucous expressiveness, and many more. Music itself is an integral part of culture, and it's been posited that our greatest musical love will always be whatever music we listened to in our late teens. I once heard some African-American friends say they'd be glad to join what's primarily an Anglo church "if they'd include some black music." In each of these areas and plenty more, we have a heart language; worship that's in something other than our heart language will require some translation work to be done, either while it's happening or in perpetual preparation as new participants are constantly brought up to speed. The church I led in Tucson from 1990–2011 intentionally offered three very distinct services to speak to different heart languages in terms of music style, degree of formality, and freedom of response. But I was in a very small minority of people who truly worshiped freely and joyfully in all three. I believe the voluntary "segregating" into different worshiping communities is more cultural than racial or ethnic, and from the city-wide vantage point of the Church, a gift, not a curse, as people have more entry points, and consequently, more people will engage.

Forever staying in our ethnic silos is not an option if we want to be the Cross culture and take unity/harmony as seriously as the New Testament does. But encouraging every congregation to become racially diverse isn't the only solution. In my experience, very few people are truly bicultural—operating with equal comfort, proficiency, and enjoyment in multiple cultures. Racially diverse congregations still only reach that one bicultural segment of the population. To expect everyone to become something they aren't runs in direct opposition to Paul's body analogy in 1 Corinthians 12. I suspect that most people choose their places of worship based on the music and what's expected of the attendees (clapping or dancing, verbal feedback expected from the audience during the message, or quiet reverence) rather than ethnicity, even though those cultural preferences have ethnic correlations.

How can we build relationships cross culturally and experience the harmony and maturity that result if congregations themselves *aren't* ethnically diverse? By finding ways for different congregations to build relationships with one another, while each congregation keeps its identity as one part of the Body of Christ. Some training on the front end will prove exceptionally helpful, so that differences are experienced as blessings and opportunities for learning. Here in Tucson we've made the most progress on this front with pastors through Pastor Prayer Summits, groups like our Pastors Partnership, and through programs that previously had been ethnically specific intentionally reaching out to invite everyone else. As pastors experience the blessings of the Cross culture, they look for ways to bless their congregations similarly. The whole concept of "domains" (introduced and discussed in Chapter 6) provides another opportunity to build bridges and learn from one another across congregations. Extended periods of time together, like the John 17 Weekends, are golden opportunities. I'll share some more possibilities at the end of the chapter.

Two days after the 2016 presidential election, Pastor Dave Goffeney of Tucson's Redemption Church hosted an event called "Tapestry: Race, Power and the Gospel." Dave is a young pastor in our community who has become a regular part of our Pastors Partnership group, and he has taken on racial reconciliation as a major theme of his congregation. Dave has shared the unique problem within his congregation: they're trying to grow older. They're looking for new attendees who *aren't* youth or young adults! At the start of the Tapestry event, he said, "We have to learn to move *toward* one another when everything in us is screaming to move away." Since most people are naturally inclined toward the path of least resistance, this will require intentionality. At that same event, Apostle Anderson said, "To deal with racism, you have to become comfortable with being uncomfortable."

Later, Pastor Wayne Wynter of Redemption Church in Phoenix taught, "The image of God is diverse. Picture God saying, 'This (all ethnicities) is how I see myself.' Loving your neighbor is a gospel issue, because the gospel affects everything. Race should be celebrated, but not worshiped." It's been said that in Heaven, the whole human race will stand before the throne together, so we probably ought to get used to the idea here on Earth. "After this I looked, and there before me was a great multitude that no one could count, from every nation, tribe, people and language, standing before the throne and before the Lamb." (Revelation 7:9)[4]

Jesus' teaching focused on the "kingdom of God," which includes but can never be reduced to the various cultures and ethnicities and political

> **BOTH THE CHURCH AND THE COMMUNITY ARE HUNGRY FOR THE LOVE FOR WHICH JESUS PRAYED IN JOHN 17.**

groups in which we find ourselves, each of which have strengths but built-in blind spots as well. Since we bring our culture with us wherever we go, usually without recognizing it, it will take intentional interaction across different cultures if we want the Cross culture we pursue to not be reduced to the traditions and values to which we happen to be accustomed.

CULTURAL ASSETS AND LIABILITIES

This section could be its own book, but since that book has already been written by others (for example, *The Culture Map: Breaking Through the Invisible Boundaries of Global Business* by Erin Meyer), I'll merely point out four significant cultural differences I've noticed in society that also impact the Church.

---

4   The concept of every nation/people group being included is not an isolated one in Revelation, but appears six different times.

Most of the time, we don't become aware of cultural differences until we stumble over them. Pastor Goffeney shared personally at Tapestry how steep his learning curve had been, and continues to be, expressing gratitude for people pointing out language and other terms that revealed biases he didn't want and hadn't noticed. He commented, "One aspect of 'white fragility' is that as Anglos we feel like we have to get it right." Humility helps us admit we've gotten it wrong in the past, likely will again in the future, but that maturity is worth the process. (Note once again: if the term "white fragility" sounds offensive, as it did to me at first, please keep reading to the end of this chapter.)

Every culture is valid—but each one also has assets and liabilities.

1. *Time.* The Anglo culture tends to value time for what it can produce; other cultures seem to value time as an investment in relationships. I first learned this on my first mission trip to Tanzania. The difference in the way time was handled between the cultures was like night and day, and I was surprised at how quickly I adjusted—and how much I liked the change! Those differences aren't just in Tanzania; they're here in Tucson, too. Running meetings cross culturally is a challenging experience when it comes to expectations about time "management" (a very Anglo concept from the outset). Just attending multicultural meetings that I'm not leading has required me to remember which "time hat" to wear in terms of expectations. Which is better, productivity or relationships? Do we really have to choose?

2. *Leadership.* The differences in leadership expectations within cultures are profound. I have always downplayed titles, especially in the congregation, out of the understanding that there's one Head of the body—and He's not me. Whenever I was asked, "What should we call you, pastor?" I always responded with, "Dave. If you really want to use a title, you can call me Pastor Dave, but Dave is just fine. If you call me Pastor Drum, I won't know what to do, and if you call me Reverend, I won't answer." But in other cultures, titles are much more significant, and by the

time I realized this, I had to ask several people if I'd offended them by calling them simply by their first names. Respect for those in authority is given much higher value in other cultures than in mine. Are there biblical pitfalls to watch out for in both approaches? Yes, there are. On the one hand, authority can be abused and never questioned; on the other hand, authority can be always questioned and rarely followed. Are there geographical and denominational influences here, too? Yes. Ethnicity isn't the only variable when it comes to the view of authority.

3. *Communication.* This probably ties back to the time issue, but my culture relies heavily on email and electronic communications. Email is virtually useless in most of my cross cultural communication. Text messages are the most universally productive form of communication I've discovered so far. I only recently learned that far more Latino churches have Facebook pages than websites. We Anglos tend to want things planned out months in advance; my Latino friends seem to be able to change the date or location of their pastor meetings a day or two ahead of time, and everybody shows up (except me, at first). Anglos like flyers and PowerPoint slides; word of mouth seems more effective in other cultures.

4. *Conflict.* I started to notice some of these distinctions through subtle observations in recent years where it was clear that communication wasn't really happening between cultures. But Erin Meyer (author of *The Culture Map*) put words to it most clearly at the 2016 Willow Creek Global Leadership Summit. Some cultures (like all Anglo cultures) use "low context" communication, meaning very few shared reference points. Low context cultures nail things down in writing. Asian cultures are the highest context communicators, with African the second highest. High context communication is sophisticated, nuanced, and layered. Until we learn to recognize and respect the differences, low context communicators think the high context folks are secretive and non-transparent, while

high context communicators think the low context folks are either not very smart or condescending. That's a sure recipe for conflict. Furthermore, some cultures prefer direct feedback while others prefer indirect. Indirect feedback cultures will use language downgraders like "kind of, sort of, possibly." Direct feedback cultures use upgraders like "absolutely." Imagine a job evaluation with an Anglo boss trying to soften the criticism and warm the room, while the Asian or African employee reads the context to mean that everything is going great, and is shocked to get a written summary afterwards identifying problems. As Pastor Goffeney said, "It's okay to not get it as long as we're humble enough to learn."

WHITE PRIVILEGE/WHITE FRAGILITY?

Honestly, I rejected these terms the first time I heard them about thirty years ago in a seminary associated with a denomination that I later helped my congregation to leave. I rejected them because I didn't trust the source—not just the person using the terms, but the entire environment I was in. My "truth radar" was on high alert, and for some good reasons, so in this arena I rejected the content not because it conflicted with biblical truth, but because it made me uncomfortable. One particular class was trying to expose racism both in culture and in theology, but I hadn't learned the individual versus systemic distinction yet. On an individual basis, I was very interested in confronting

> TO DEAL WITH RACISM, YOU HAVE TO BECOME COMFORTABLE WITH BEING UNCOMFORTABLE.

any racist tendencies I noticed in myself, and voluntarily signed up to march in a protest over some Klan activity that had resulted in multiple injuries during what should have been a peaceful Dr. Martin Luther King Jr. march. The images from that protest march in Forsythe County, Georgia in 1987 are still clearly seared into my mind. But when it came to systemic issues, it sounded too much like politics from the other party, so I opted out and shut down.

The dear friends I've made in the last six years, and the depth of the relationships which has invited uncomfortable conversations, have made it possible to reexamine topics I previously dismissed. As I mentioned before, it takes something bigger than the gap to bridge the gap, and our unity in Christ creates a Cross culture that is both undeniable and bigger than the racial/political gap.

"White privilege" refers to some privileges we Anglos receive in our country simply because of being the majority culture. For example, we'll get the benefit of the doubt with the police far more often than our other-than-white sisters and brothers. When incarceration rates *for the same crime* are dramatically higher for persons of color than for Anglos, that's white privilege.[5] There are multiple factors involved— with differences in education, income, broken families—but regardless of the cause, the reality that Anglos start off with an advantage is what's referred to as white privilege. "White fragility," quite simply, refers to the various ways we Anglos might deny or deflect the concept of white privilege, refusing to acknowledge or take responsibility for systemic problems. Returning to 1 Corinthians 12:26, regardless of what it's called, our inability to suffer with those who suffer is a problem that can't be ignored. Bishop T.D. Jakes shared at the 2016 Global Leadership Summit, "Systemic racism isn't about whether you like the color of somebody or not. It is whether you have included them in the strategy for success." The goal isn't for the more privileged group to "rescue" the less privileged one. The goal is to come alongside one another—to be the Cross culture—so that everyone has the opportunity to be part of the solution.

At the Tapestry event, Apostle Anderson was asked to comment on white fragility. His suggestion: "Start with prayer. Allow God to strengthen you, to give you grace, to accept you unconditionally as you are. He hasn't given us a spirit of fear. If our identity is in Christ, there's nothing to prove and nobody to impress." At that same event, Pastor Aaron Dailey (the Anglo pastor whose co-pastor is African-American

---

5   Google "incarceration rates by race" and pick from any number of studies.

Wayne Wynter, quoted earlier) directly taught on the topic. Here are my notes from that event:

> There's something in us that makes us want to think we deserve what we have. The moment you admit your white privilege, you have responsibilities. 1 Corinthians 4:7 says "What do you have that you didn't receive?" And the parable of the talents clearly reveals that we don't all start with the same gifts. The biggest problem is our individualism: we try to justify ourselves individually as not racist. We're so concerned with personal justification that we ignore the sin in our world.

What's the solution? In Philippians 2, the Bible clearly states that Jesus had *all* the power and privilege, and yet He emptied himself. The question isn't if we have privilege—it's how we use it. How can we use the gifts/blessings/privilege we've received to come alongside our sisters and brothers? The answer to white privilege isn't white guilt. The questions of "Where do I start?" and "What can I do?" are white questions! We want to fix things. To start, simply enter into the brokenness. Be there and listen.

Guilt isn't the goal.[6] Each ethnicity was created by God and reflects His image. When the dominant ethnicity in a culture brings with it an unequal portion of privileges, the culture of the Cross invites us to empty ourselves of our privileges, like Jesus did, and use our blessings to bless others. Bill and Martha Wills, leaders of the Racial Reconciliation Network (founded by their son, the late Bishop Ollie Wills) shared in their 2016 Christmas card, "We must realize that we are interdependent upon each other; we do not have the full counsel of God by ourselves; and we have spiritual resources among ourselves that can and will benefit each other."

MOST OF THE TIME, WE DON'T BECOME AWARE OF CULTURAL DIFFERENCES UNTIL WE STUMBLE OVER THEM.

---

6   Neither is shame. Different cultures tend toward one or the other: guilt or shame.

RACIAL RECONCILERS: BECOMING A CROSS CULTURE

Here are some tools and perspectives that have proven enormously helpful in creating the Cross culture we're now experiencing at previously unknown levels for our city.

- *Time.* Time for many is our most precious resource, so giving the gift of time to empty ourselves is a Cross culture act. The statement we probably make more than any other at 4Tucson is, "It's all about relationships, and there's no shortcut to relationships." They take time. The larger the block of time, the better. One three-day Pastor Prayer Summit can accomplish far more than three one-day Pastor Prayer Summits. During the John 17 Weekends in 2016, one African-American woman, Rose Tederous, came to the weekend quite bruised and battered over all the racial tension in the country. Several Dallas police officers had just been killed that week in retaliation for multiple incidences of police violence around the country. She was concerned that she was going to be the only black woman in attendance that weekend. Furthermore, she had just lost a dear friend to death the day the retreat was to begin, so she had several built-in excuses not to attend. Regardless, she was convinced that God was telling her she needed to be there. She wrote up an amazing testimony about the experience[7] and here are her concluding sentences after spending 72 hours in a unified and very diverse body of Christ: "Because I matter to Jesus, I now feel the strength to fight injustice as a whole person, not as a broken person. With this knowledge and Jesus as my guide, I can fight injustice with love."

- *Story.* In our Pastors Partnership group, one of the most powerful things we did the first year was to give a couple of people a chance to share their stories in each meeting. It may have been their story of how they came to faith in Jesus, their call to ministry, and how their story intersected with the topics of

---

7   See Appendix 1.

race and culture. One of the things my daughter and son-in-law (staff workers with InterVarsity) struggled with as they went through cross cultural training was that they'd never thought much about their own culture. "Do we even have a culture?" is not an uncommon question for Anglos—partly because the dominant culture is likely to be less aware of their distinctions, and partly because Anglos view things more individually than collectively to begin with.

OUR UNITY IN CHRIST CREATES A CROSS CULTURE THAT IS BOTH UNDENIABLE AND BIGGER THAN THE RACIAL/POLITICAL GAP.

As the stories were shared in the Pastors Partnership group, it was incredibly enlightening to hear how concepts I might have read about had been personally experienced by brothers across the table. We saw movies together that addressed racial themes like *42* (the Jackie Robinson Story) and discussed them afterwards. As we began to talk about how to bring our congregations into these discussions, we offered movies with popcorn and small group discussions afterward to our entire congregations, using the motion pictures *Selma* and *Woodlawn* as two examples. The response was both large in numbers and universally positive. As our stories are shared, they cross and intersect, and the Cross culture takes deeper root.

- *Walk across the bridge.* Don't begin by creating an event and inviting others from another race to join you; find an event that they've created and join *them*. Speaking especially to my Anglo brothers and sisters, we're used to leading and being in charge. Someone once said, "If you're in a room with mixed ethnicities, watch how often those of color will defer to the Anglos, and how often the Anglos will lead." Yet when we join, support, and celebrate something somebody else started and is leading, we honor them in impactful ways. When we engage in the culture of the Cross, we cross bridges by leaving our comfort zones and entering someone else's neighborhood.

- *"Help me understand."* That simple sentence is gold in reconciling racial distance and differences. If the Cross culture could have a slogan, this might be it. "Help me understand your experience of racial profiling." "Help me understand what's happening in the riots." "Help me understand how you're choosing to vote the way you are." "Help me understand what it's like to be an immigrant."

  Cole Brown wrote a powerful admonition to us Anglos after the Ferguson tension blew up. Here's part of it: "Until you have listened to your black brothers and sisters tell you dozens upon dozens of stories of their experiences; until you have seen the look of despair in their eyes as they tell them; until you have wept bitter tears over the pain in their voice—I beg you not to speak on this situation. It doesn't even matter if you are right or wrong. It matters that you are speaking without the empathy and humility the gospel produces. You are hurting God's people. You are hurting God's name. Reason with me—at the very least, isn't it possible, just possible—that your brothers and sisters of color see some things that you can't see? Experience some things that you can't experience? After all, they live every day of their lives in a skin you have never worn and can never wear. Isn't it at least reasonable to believe that they might have a more accurate view of what living in that skin is like in America than you do? Humility calls for you to listen to their voices, listen to their experiences, and to care more about their good and their concerns than your own."

- *Humility.* Brown mentioned it in his comments, and I've come to believe it's the key to the entire topic of unity/harmony. I don't have all the answers; humility acknowledges that fact while pride denies it. Here are three postures that humility takes in the relationship building process of racial reconciliation. 1) As we enter into cross cultural relationships, our humility calls on us to be aware, sensitive, and to prayerfully work to avoid giving offense by the words, actions, and attitudes we either engage in or refrain from. 2) Humility calls on us to enter into relationships actively despite the likelihood that we'll cause offense at some point unintentionally. We expect to apologize when it happens and grow through the experience. 3) As our relationships and trust grow, humility helps us offer the other person the benefit of the doubt, as a brother or sister in Christ and a person of good will, so that we choose not to take offense at offensive things. Jesus prayed from the cross, "Father, forgive them, for they do not know what they are doing." (Luke 23:34) Humility creates the Cross culture we need.

HARMONY TO THE TUNE OF RACE

As followers of Christ, our goal is to approach things not primarily from an ethnic perspective, but from a Kingdom perspective that personifies the Cross culture. Our ethnicity is part of who we are—part of who God created us to be. It's a gift and the perspectives that come with it need to be shared. But our primary lens isn't our cultural lens, it's our Kingdom lens, viewing everything through the cross of Jesus the King. As a Latino brother shared in one of our immigration conversations, "My ethnicity didn't die for me; Jesus did."

HUMILITY CREATES THE CROSS CULTURE WE NEED.

The Cross culture is the best path I know toward racial reconciliation. It's one of the sweetest melodies to be found, one the world desperately seeks, and one the gospel can uniquely empower. It is poetically communicated in this song written by Trinity Vineyard from the album *Prayers of the Saints*, based on the Prayer of St. Francis, a regular in my family's house of worship.

Make me an instrument of peace
Where there is hate let me sow love
Where there is hurt let me bring Your healing

Make me an instrument of peace
Where there is fear let faith arise
Where there is dark let me be Your light

Make of me, Your hands and feet
I want to be, to the people around me
What You want to be, to the people around me

It's in the loving we find love
It's in the giving we receive
It's in the dying we are found

If it's truly all about relationship, and relationships take time, and relationships with those whose culture and experience vary dramatically from ours virtually guarantee conflict, there's another key ingredient we'll need in order to travel through the bumps to the blessings. That's where we turn next.

QUESTIONS FOR SELF-REFLECTION

- What challenges you the most about both this topic and this chapter? What do you plan to do about it?

- What blessings have you received from leaving your comfort zone and building relationships with people very different from you?

- When is comfort from the Comforter, the Holy Spirit, and when is comfort simply a tool the enemy uses that's based in fear, a tool designed to keep us from moving and growing? How do you know when the Holy Spirit is calling you out of your comfort zone?

- Which of the cultural assets and liabilities were most insightful for you?

- Which of the "racial reconcilers" is God inviting you to employ?

TODAY'S GPS

Lord and Savior Jesus, we honor and praise You for the risky decision You undertook to take on flesh fully and completely, such that You were Jewish by ethnicity and first-century Palestinian by culture, even though You transcend both. Triune God, when You look in the mirror You don't see one color but all, one culture but many, and we look forward to the day when people of every race and culture gather around Your throne on equal and level footing. Protect us from the enemy who loves to sow division and mistrust, to cause us to rehash wounds rather than heal from them, and who fans misunderstanding into hatred. Sanctify us, Jesus—thank You for showing us grace in our brokenness and failures. Help us do the same for one another, for Your sake, our sake, and the sake of our country and world. Amen.

Chapter Five

DIVORCE IS NOT AN OPTION: LESSONS FROM MARRIAGE

IF marriage was easy, the divorce rate wouldn't be so high. The number of Millennials avoiding marriage altogether wouldn't keep growing. Our culture wouldn't be hemorrhaging on so many fronts due to broken families. Yet if there is any area where Satan works harder against unity/harmony and identity than in marriages, it is in his "divide and conquer" strategy employed against the Church, the family of God.

As we learned in Chapter 1, Jesus was hardly haphazard when the second of His three supporting petitions to unity/harmony was "protection from the outside." The enemy wins when he blows up all or part of a church family in a flashy, sometimes public meltdown. But he also wins when he convinces us that a quiet, maybe even "respectful" divorce is an option in the City Church, as if the principle of love another and unity/harmony isn't that big of a deal anyway. Besides, God regularly brings new life out of the embers of broken relationships. Why not give Him another opportunity?

4Tucson is built on Jesus' John 17 prayer. We believe that unity/ harmony isn't the end, it's the means to the end—and that end is twofold: that everyone watching comes to know the love of God (John 17:23) and that the city itself is transformed to the glory of God (Jeremiah 29:7). Every Wednesday morning, we have a staff meeting where directors of each of the domains as well as the other newer departments meet together. One of the traditions we've intentionally built into our 4Tucson internal culture is practicing "love one another" within our own staff. As one example, every birthday gets acknowledged with an around-the-horn celebration of the birthday man or woman, with each one of us sharing a couple of things about the honoree that they love and are thankful for to the Lord. As proof that we've made progress in not being clones of one another who all excel in the same areas and share the same personalities, a fair portion of people in the room find this practice incredibly uncomfortable. When we celebrated two birthdays at the same meeting, a rarity for our small staff, the love fest finally ended after 45 minutes— and several comments were made about what the precious gift our 4Tucson family has become.

> I DON'T THINK WE CAN CITE IRRECONCILABLE DIFFERENCES AS A REASON FOR GIVING UP ANY MORE THAN I CAN DO THAT WITH MY WIFE.

But here's the deal: if it wasn't for the Bible's marriage analogy, that day might never have arrived. In Ephesians 5:21–33, the Apostle Paul compares marriage between a husband and wife to the relationship between Christ and His bride, the Church. God used that comparison for us to keep the train from completely coming off the tracks.

THE DAY(S) THE DREAM NEARLY DIED

As citywide Christian unity/harmony in Tucson grew, so did the opportunities in front of our organization to make even more of an impact. When I wrote *Jesus' Surprising Strategy* in 2013, 4Tucson didn't have any departments; we hadn't yet evolved to that level. As God blessed us and helped us expand, the need for specialization grew as well. We needed specialists in areas like communication, databases, overall visioning, partner support, organizational management, and so forth. Those areas may not have sounded as exciting as being a domain director, but they were absolutely necessary. Human bodies don't do very well without skeletons. When you look at a body, it's not the skeleton you want to see; if bones are showing, that's a problem in and of itself. But the body isn't going anywhere without a skeleton supporting it.

As 4Tucson evolved, each one of us had to daily discern what our "lane" was and how to stay in it. Swerving all over the road was not an option. Newer additions to the team were required who weren't generalists but specialists, with well-honed skill sets and perspectives that accompanied their areas of specialty. Communication within our team became simultaneously more essential and more challenging. Trust and mutual submission was required for each person to play their part without inefficient overlap, but trust and mutual submission could only grow out of relationships, and there was no shortcut to relationships. The watching world hadn't hit "pause" while we were trying to work out our internal systems; they kept clamoring for more visible unity/harmony in action—and the pressure was on to deliver.

Because the pedal was to the metal on several fronts, sparks were flying. Each of our leaders brought their own perspectives to the needs at hand, but those perspectives were often dissimilar. Communication wasn't prioritized to the degree required, and so trust was starting to break down. Each come-to-Jesus meeting one week seemed to be followed by another the next week that was even more intense and with even higher stakes. A therapist could have had a field day just by observing everyone's body language. This season continued for nearly six months.

Were the conflicts due to human sin and blind spots, or the enemy attempting to divide and conquer? Yes to both. Could the conflicts have been avoided with more prayer protection from the enemy and more spiritual growth and maturity on the part of each team member? Yes for most of them, but some of the conflicts were probably unavoidable and in reality the only path forward.

In one of those difficult meetings, one of our original four domain directors, Brian Goodall, said, "I don't think God wants us to blow up. I don't think we can cite irreconcilable differences as a reason for giving up any more than I can do that with my wife. I gave up that option at the altar."

Did Brian's comment resolve the conflicts? Not immediately, as our challenging season lasted a few more months after he made his statement. But God brought his insight to mind more than once in the months that followed, closing down the all-too-attractive path of least resistance known as "bailing out." More than once, some macabre humor surfaced in tongue-in-cheek suggestions like, "Let's go start a 5Tucson, which will be one better than 4Tucson," reminding us of how ridiculous—or blasphemous—that would appear. More than once, God caused us to remember that while He's always bigger than our rebellion and failure, there were situations where the costs of our rebellion and failure could take out an entire generation (see Numbers 13–14). Entities that for decades had ignored the Church in Tucson were now turning to the Church, and if the organization particularly tasked with uniting/harmonizing the city's Body of Christ imploded, it could be a generation or more before similar seasons of harvest returned.

Through that time of discontent, all of us at 4Tucson learned that for the Proverbs 27:17 truth of iron sharpening iron to work, those involved in the process must be diverse, the relationships must be strong, the conversations must be honest, and the commitment must be enduring. And, thanks to Brian's wisdom, we understood that divorce was not an option—as an organization or for individuals in the organization. "Til death do us part" applied to citywide Christian unity/harmony as well as it did to marriage.

JOHN 17 AGAIN AND AGAIN

We know that Jesus prayed for unity/harmony in John 17, but is that prayer isolated or is it a central theme that the entire New Testament takes seriously? We're already seen how John 17 unity/harmony is the main thrust of 1 Corinthians 12 from which the Body of Christ analogy is most completely developed, and that Ephesians 4 is all about how unity leads to maturity and central to the letter to the Christians in the city of Ephesus. We've also learned that James 5, Hebrews 6, Colossians 2, and Philippians 2 carry powerful messages about unity/harmony. But once I started trying to take unity/harmony as seriously as Jesus did, I didn't have to go looking for other New Testament references in addition to those. They seemed to find me virtually every time I opened the Bible.

> SOMETIMES
> WE HOLD HANDS;
> OTHER TIMES,
> WE JUST HOLD ON.

- Romans 13:9–10: "The commandments, 'You shall not commit adultery,' 'You shall not murder,' 'You shall not steal,' 'You shall not covet,' and whatever other command there may be, are summed up in this one command: 'Love your neighbor as yourself.' [10]Love does no harm to a neighbor. Therefore love is the fulfillment of the law."

- 2 Corinthians 8:24: "Therefore show these men the proof of your love and the reason for our pride in you, so that the churches can see it."

- Galatians 5:14: "For the entire law is fulfilled in keeping this one command: 'Love your neighbor as yourself.'"

- 1 Thessalonians 3:12–13: "May the Lord make your love increase and overflow for each other and for everyone else, just as ours does for you. [13]May he strengthen your hearts so that you will be blameless and holy in the presence of our God and Father when our Lord Jesus comes with all his holy ones."

- 1 Thessalonians 4:9–10 shows the importance of loving all the believers in the region, and "to do so more and more."

- 2 Thessalonians 1:3: "We ought always to thank God for you, brothers and sisters, and rightly so, because your faith is growing more and more, and the love all of you have for one another is increasing."

- 1 Timothy 1:5 says, "The goal of this command is love..." (The command was to teach truth and confront falsehood.)

- Hebrews 12:14–15: "Make every effort to live in peace with everyone and to be holy; without holiness no one will see the Lord. ¹⁵See to it that no one falls short of the grace of God and that no bitter root grows up to cause trouble and defile many."

- 1 Peter 1:22: "Now that you have purified yourselves by obeying the truth so that you have sincere love for each other, love one another deeply, from the heart."

- 1 Peter 2:17: "Show proper respect to everyone, love the family of believers, fear God, honor the emperor."

- 1 Peter 3:8: "Finally, all of you, be like-minded, be sympathetic, love one another, be compassionate and humble."

- 1 Peter 4:7–8: "The end of all things is near. Therefore be alert and of sober mind so that you may pray. ⁸Above all, love each other deeply, because love covers over a multitude of sins."

- 2 Peter 1:7–9 says to supplement your faith with "godliness, mutual affection; and to mutual affection, love. ⁸For if you possess these qualities in increasing measure, they will keep you from being ineffective and unproductive in your knowledge of our Lord Jesus Christ. ⁹But whoever does not have them is nearsighted and blind, forgetting that they have been cleansed from their past sins."

- Jude 19 makes clear that the godless men addressed throughout the letter are "people who divide you." The doxology in Jude 24–25 gives praise to the God who can mature us.

Not surprisingly, John, who included Jesus' prayer for unity/harmony in his Gospel account, also included it in his other New Testament books, too.[1] Unity/harmony is arguably the main point of 1 John (see especially 2:7 and 4:7–21) and it's clearly the main point of the two short letters of 2 John and 3 John.

By my count, that means that at least 18 of the 22 New Testament letters address unity/harmony, in several cases as the main point of the letter. All the New Testament letter writers (Paul, James, Peter, John, and Jude) speak to the topic.

Why did John include Jesus' prayer in his Gospel while Matthew, Mark, and Luke did not? I don't know the answer to that, but Matthew, Mark, and Luke each record "love for God" and "love for neighbor" as the central two-part command upon which the entire Old Testament is built. Each Gospel writer was impacted by Jesus' teaching on the topic, even if John was the only one to record Jesus' prayer. John's Gospel was the last of the four to be written, so perhaps by the time he wrote his Gospel and letters he already noticed how "if it was easy, Jesus wouldn't have prayed for it."

If experience from the last several years weren't enough to convince me, a reexamination of the New Testament did it. The conclusions are stark and convicting. We don't prioritize our relationships with fellow believers to the degree that the Bible does. As a result, we remain childish when God expects us to mature. We miss out on the blessings we could receive from fellow sisters and brothers in Christ. Isolated body parts accomplish a fraction of what the entire unified body could—and

---

1   With the exception of Revelation, unless 2:4 includes love for people, which it very well might.

the world misses out on its best opportunity to come to know the love of God.

By closing the escape route in advance for times when conflict becomes painful and challenging, everybody wins. We grow and stretch and learn in ways only conflict itself can produce. I'm certain there will be more painful challenges at 4Tucson to practice what we preach. But had we bailed when the going got tough, everyone would've lost: "us" and "them."

THE BRIDE OF CHRIST'S WEDDING VOWS

Jesus regularly referred to His relationship with His followers as being similar to that of a bridegroom and a bride. Additionally, four times in the last chapters of the Bible, Revelation 19–22, the Church is called Jesus' bride. What can we learn about citywide unity/harmony from traditional wedding vows?

- *From this day forward.* When we sign up as followers of Christ, whether we know it or not, we're making vows to one another that are as significant as the vows made to our husband or wife. "Whoever claims to love God yet hates a brother or sister is a liar. For whoever does not love their brother and sister, whom they have seen, cannot love God, whom they have not seen." (1 John 4:20) "No one has ever seen God; but if we love one another, God lives in us and his love is made complete in us." (1 John 4:12)

> IT'S HUMBLING TO ADMIT OUR NEED FOR OTHERS AND WHAT OTHERS CAN BRING— AND THAT'S WHY IT'S ESSENTIAL.

- *To have and to hold.* Having the kind of unity-not-uniformity for which Jesus prayed is a sweet, sweet thing. Holding on to it requires commitment. My beautiful bride and I were married on July 9, 1988. Sometimes we hold hands; other times, we just hold on. But when we committed to have one another, we knew we were committed to hold on, come what may. That commitment time and again has helped us learn what we needed to learn during the stormy seasons, which then gave way to sweet seasons of marital joy, deeper even than the time before. The same dynamic will occur in your relationships with your brothers and sisters in Christ—so long as you hold on to them.

- *For better, for worse.* Part of the power of this wedding vow is that from day one, even starry-eyed brides and grooms acknowledge (if they are listening) that marriage isn't a fairy tale; it's real life. Parents that protect their kids from ever seeing a squabble do them a disservice. If you never saw your parents fight, you may have thought the world was coming to an end the first time you and your spouse did, which might well have been on your honeymoon. As Christians, then, if we are truly walking across the room in the city to the parts that are significantly divergent from us, we should expect conflict. Commit to not bail out before the blessing that comes through a "for better, for worse" commitment.

- *For richer, for poorer.* Jesus tells uncomfortable stories about the kingdom of God that don't sound very fair by human standards. Not everyone gets the same gifts, not everyone starts at the same place, and not everyone receives the same praise. If we are comparing ourselves to one another, we'll quickly discover that jealousy is a relationship killer, both in marriage and in city-wide unity/harmony. As I've shared with countless brides and grooms on their wedding day, we're never closer to one another than when Jesus is right between us. Jesus is the head of the body; we're all just different parts with unique functions that we alone are equipped to carry out.

- *In plenty and in want.* Most Christians I know love to serve and help others, but have a much harder time receiving those same blessings from others. We must learn the steps to both sides of the dance because God has designed us to be both giver and recipient. When Jesus was serving by washing the feet of a decidedly uncomfortable Peter, He said, "Unless I wash you, you have no part with me." (John 13:8) It's humbling to admit our need for others and what others can bring—and that's why it's essential. Different parts of the Citywide Church can truly help one another in significant ways, but only if we learn to know one another, trust one another, and give and receive from one another.

- *In joy and in sorrow.* When one part of the Body of Christ rejoices, we all rejoice together—which means there are always reasons to rejoice! Our problem is we don't know one another well enough to know the reasons. I've heard people say they might only personally know one or two people they'd consider heroes of the faith; I know dozens of them, and meet with them every week! Angels are in a constant state of rejoicing (Luke 15:7, 10) over everyday activity in the Body of Christ around the city— and we will be, too, when we develop and nurture relationships. At the same time, there will also be opportunities to comfort and grieve. When a well-known African-American pastor in our community died unexpectedly, the Cross culture relationships that had been built enabled his memorial service to be held in a predominantly Anglo church led by a friend, and the congregation that gathered reflected well the environment our dear friend was already experiencing in Heaven.

- *In sickness and in health.* The people Jesus calls us to love are sick with the disease called sin, and so are we! If it weren't for sinners, there wouldn't be anyone to fill any of our congregations. Sin sickness shouldn't shock us to the degree that it does. Realistic expectations can go a long way to lessening the drama that surrounds conflict. Blind spots abound, and praise God when we're privileged to come to know someone else well enough for us to see theirs and them to see ours. Jesus is the great physician, and we'll see sickness give way to health more often as the body grows in its infinite connections to one another and maturity becomes the outcome.

- *To love and to cherish.* Webster Dictionary defines "cherish" as to hold dear, to feel or show affection for, to keep or cultivate with care and affection, or to entertain or harbor in the mind deeply and resolutely. Every aspect of that definition applies to citywide unity/harmony. These last several years of commitment to one another in the Citywide Church have led to countless

> WHAT BETTER PLACE TO LEARN HOW TO BE RELATIONAL THAN IN A COMMUNITY WHERE CONFESSION AND FORGIVENESS ARE AT THE HEART OF OUR IDENTITY?

relationships that are dear, affectionate, and held onto deeply and resolutely. When Christ followers in our city think about what we were missing before, we have no intention of returning to the days of "everyone did what was right in his own eyes." (Judges 21:25, NASB)

AS LONG AS WE BOTH SHALL LIVE?

How far can we really push the marriage analogy in relation to unity/ harmony in the Body of Christ? In Malachi 2:16 (NASB), God says, "I hate divorce." Is the same true for fractured unity/harmony between brothers and sisters in Christ? When Paul and Barnabas split after years of beautiful harmony enjoyed by two people whose giftings and personalities couldn't have been much more different from one another, I wonder if the angels in Heaven wept.

Let's see what we can learn by applying unity/harmony to the City Church, recognizing that not every movement of staff or participants from one congregation to another is problematic.

1. *At a congregational level.* I previously mentioned the classes I held
    regularly at my congregation called "Christian Appetizers" for
    those either exploring Christianity or expressing a desire to join
    our congregation. I intentionally separated the commitment
    to participate in the group from the commitment to join the
    congregation. Toward the end of the class, we talked about our
    congregations' beliefs and values, as well as discussed how we
    defined partnership (our term for membership.) I always said,
    "Date our congregation for as long as you want. You're welcome
    to participate in our congregations' activities whether you've
    made a partnership commitment or not. But I encourage you
    at some point to consider making a commitment, which we'll
    be making to you as well. There comes a point in a relation-
    ship where the commitment is what helps it keep growing; the
    relationship will stagnate without that commitment. If it hasn't
    already happened, the day will come when I'll disappoint or frus-
    trate you, as will the congregation. We're all sinners, so know
    that on the front end. It's our commitment to one another that
    will carry us through when that happens. Rather than bailing out
    in the midst of the conflict, we're making a commitment to do
    everything possible to work it out." I usually continued by shar-
    ing my belief that the immaturity of American Christianity was
    largely due to our low level of commitment to God and each
    other. When the going gets tough, the tough usually get going—
    right on out the door to the next congregation. Our consumer
    approach to Christianity is killing us, since we approach congre-
    gational life with the same level of loyalty as we give to fast
    food restaurants.

    How does a change of reference in 1 Corinthians 12 from
    the Body of Christ as the local congregation to the Body of
    Christ as the citywide church affect my congregational-partner-
    ship view? Rather than contradict the perspective, it adds to it.
    Lone Ranger Christianity, while the religion of choice in America,
    is entirely foreign to the New Testament. The Christian journey
    is inherently relational and has been from the beginning. Now

retired longtime Tucson Pastor Roger Barrier was the first one I heard point out that even in the perfection of the Garden of Eden, before sin entered the picture, God said, "It is not good for man to be alone." The necessity for relationship is biblically undeniable, with over 50 "one another" commandments in the New Testament,[2] and the best place to learn and practice these commandments is the local congregation. Relationships indeed must be learned because many people didn't have great relationship building modeled during their childhood. A group of people who are committed to the same ultimate goal (following Jesus) can be a phenomenal place to develop people skills. I've frequently read articles saying that regardless of the industry, people skills are the most sought-after quality in employees, and the lack of them the biggest reason for dismissal. Relationship skills are a vanishing art with the ever-increasing pace of our culture combined with the move toward more electronic communication. What better place to learn how to be relational than in a community where confession and forgiveness are at the heart of our identity?

A well-established statistic is that the divorce rate for second, third, and subsequent marriages is significantly higher than for first marriages. My best guess why is that the constant in all marriages is *us!* God is very generous, and when we fail a test the first time, we get multiple opportunities to retake it until we pass. The maturing that could have happened by working through the conflicts the first time around is still needed. There are plenty of relational lessons that can only be learned by pressing on and pressing through. Humility is high on that list.

When is it appropriate for church attendees or staff to move from one congregation to another? I reserve the right to disagree later with what I think at this moment, so consider this another conversation starter.

---

2   Discussed in Chapter 6 of *Jesus' Surprising Strategy*, and listed in the Appendix.

Good reasons for moving on:
- Launching a new ministry/congregation
- Geographical change, desire to be part of a congregation in the neighborhood
- Individual gifts can be better utilized in another setting

Bad reasons for moving on:
- Easier to avoid addressing a conflict
- Somebody sinned, causing hurt and pain
- Desire to stay comfortable

Good methods for moving on:
- After prayer and conversation with trusted friends who will speak the truth
- After conversation with leadership
- Being launched, prayed over, celebrated for the next chapter

Bad methods for moving on:
- Out of anger and hurt
- Trying to convince others to come with you
- Without prayer, conversation with trusted friends who will speak the truth, or conversation with leadership

2. *At a citywide level.* Sometimes what feels like division is actually multiplication. Even when God didn't orchestrate the division because some combination of human sin and the enemy's effort was behind it, God can use the division to create multiplication. He did this repeatedly in the book of Acts. For many years, I was so focused as a pastor on helping my congregation grow, I tried to hold on to people as if they

NOT EVERY MOVEMENT OF STAFF OR PARTICIPANTS FROM ONE CONGREGATION TO ANOTHER IS PROBLEMATIC.

were mine, or at least belonged to our congregation. Some of this was rooted in sinful competition and pride. Other instances may not have had sinful motivation, but still grew out of an incomplete picture of a citywide church.

When congregations and pastors learn to trust one another, we more frequently see good reasons and methods for moving than bad reasons and methods. Pastors can aid a "church shopper" by asking some good questions about their last experience, sometimes encouraging them to go back and either work through the issues or at least leave in better shape. For any number of reasons, sometimes a fresh start in a new setting can be helpful. The more our commitment to one another and trust of one another grows in the City Church, the more often painful divisions can be avoided altogether—and among those that still happen, many can be turned into healthy multiplications.

Trust at a citywide level in the Body of Christ is incredibly challenging. What sometimes gets called "citywide" is in actuality a small segment of the city, a denominational or ethnic slice of the pie. The tendency to affiliate with like-minded people is entirely human and not completely negative. Without a strong wind of the Holy Spirit bringing to mind the words and prayer of Jesus, each congregation, network/denomination, culture, and generation will tend to primarily stay in its own silo. It takes a great degree of intentionality to work toward true collaboration on a citywide level, where the strengths and differences from all the various perspectives within the Body of Christ are brought to the same table on equal footing. For success to be broadly achieved, a tremendous commitment to unity is truly required.

Many who have studied effective congregations have noted the value of lengthy pastorates. I'm convinced part of the reason for this is that relationships take time, and long-tenured leaders have an opportunity to work through some of the long-standing challenges and blind spots within the congregation. For true citywide transformation to take place, the need for lengthy pastorates is even greater. Not only can they produce healthy congregations, relationships *between leaders from different congregations* take even more time and intentionality. When conflict arises (and it will if we ever get close enough to one another to truly collaborate), true breakthrough in some of the city's strongholds requires the twin-fold commitment to truth and unity that took Jesus to His knees. Similar to what we experienced in the 4Tucson staff, individuals and leaders across the city are called to a place where they say to one another, "I know you love the Lord like I do and want the same things for our city that I do. We're not seeing eye to eye right now, but breaking fellowship is not an option. Regardless of how many painful conversations it takes, Jesus is praying that we stick it out until we can truly understand where others are coming from, and probably come to understand things both of us are missing. I'd rather align myself with Jesus' prayer than go my own way. I love you, and we're stuck with each other!"

THE MINISTRY OF RECONCILIATION

In the Lord's Prayer, we pray for God's kingdom to come on Earth as it is in Heaven. But we're still here on Earth for the time being—and sometimes marriages are so broken that divorce is the best in a series of bad options. Likewise, the longer I work for John 17 in my own city, the more stories I hear of pain and brokenness. You may have heard of "splants"—church splits that resulted in the planting of another congregation. There are instances of broken trust where a leader appears to have abused the confidence of a congregation or senior leader for personal gain. Sometimes several pastors or congregations have agreed to collaborate on a citywide project, only to have one end up shouldering an unequal portion of the responsibility in dollars, personnel, or time. Congregations or pastors can split the unity/truth dialogue, choosing one over the other and ending up preaching intentionally or subconsciously against their fellow brothers and sisters in Christ, literally or through their actions. Sins of omission and sins of commission; unhealthy pastors and unhealthy congregations; individual sin (person against person) and collective sin (group against group)—all these and more can leave behind multiple casualties whose ability to trust is damaged. These hurts must be addressed before the people involved will jump into the next call for a John 17 gala in the city.

Jesus taught in Matthew 5:23–24, "Therefore, if you are offering your gift at the altar and there remember that your brother or sister has something against you, ²⁴leave your gift there in front of the altar. First go and be reconciled to them; then come and offer your gift." There's no indication that Jesus was thinking narrowly, referencing only conflict within a family or congregation. His directive is all-encompassing.

Second Corinthians 5:16–21 will need to be taken seriously by church leaders in any community who are calling for commitment to one another in Christ that resembles marital commitment.

"So from now on we regard no one from a worldly point of view. Though we once regarded Christ in this way, we do so no longer. ¹⁷Therefore, if anyone is in Christ, the new creation has come: The old has gone, the new is here! ¹⁸All this is from God, who reconciled us to himself through Christ and gave us the ministry of reconciliation: ¹⁹that God was reconciling the world to himself in Christ, not counting people's sins against them. And he has committed to us the message of reconciliation. ²⁰We are therefore Christ's ambassadors, as though God were making his appeal through us. We implore you on Christ's behalf: Be reconciled to God. ²¹God made him who had no sin to be sin for us, so that in him we might become the righteousness of God."

WHEN CONGREGATIONS AND PASTORS LEARN TO TRUST ONE ANOTHER, WE MORE FREQUENTLY SEE GOOD REASONS AND METHODS FOR MOVING THAN BAD.

Each of us can play a role in being peacemakers, assisting those who need to mourn, and then going together to the cross from which confession and forgiveness flow. Trusted Christian counselors in the city can play vital roles in helping individuals and leaders work through their bruises, callouses, and broken bones.

Ecclesiastes 4:12 is often used as a wedding text. Pastor Angel Morfin and I taught a group of Hispanic pastors on the topic of "Better Together: Common Ground" and Angel presented a marvelous exposition of verses 9–12:

> Two are better than one because
> they have a good return for their labor:
> ¹⁰If either of them falls down,
> one can help the other up.
> But pity anyone who falls
> and has no one to help them up.
> ¹¹Also, if two lie down together,
> they will keep warm.
> But how can one keep warm alone?
> ¹²Though one may be overpowered,
> two can defend themselves.
> A cord of three strands
> is not quickly broken.

Angel pointed out the blessings in each verse: greater productivity (vs. 9); assistance when we fall (vs. 10); companionship (vs. 11); and protection in battle (vs. 12). The enemy's motive is to divide; Jesus' motive is to reconcile. We can be part of the solution through prayer and peacemaking.

If it was easy, the attending joy wouldn't be so significant when deep unity is accomplished on Earth as it is in Heaven.

THE DANCE OF UNITY

All of my kids are into music (their mom, after all, is a music educator) and some will occasionally record themselves singing multiple parts of the same song, one vocal overlaid on top of the other. Blending vocal qualities together is much easier if you're the one singing all of the parts. The outcome is beautiful, too!

I'm sure with today's technology there's a way to video yourself dancing both parts and "splicing" it together so that you're dancing with yourself. Yet I'm not sure the image of dancing with yourself is all that desirable. Something about

> **ABSENCE OF CONFLICT ISN'T THE GOAL, BUT RATHER THE MIND OF CHRIST AND A MUTUAL RECOGNITION OF OUR CONTINUAL NEED FOR GRACE.**

dance suggests that your partner needs to be different from you. Dance, then, is a rich word choice for the biblical concept of unity/harmony in the Body of Christ where many very different parts form one cohesive, coordinated whole.

Where is unity/harmony the most challenging? In the closest of relationships. Lifelong marriage requires daily adjustment and sacrifice. Kids form a welcome intrusion into the marital dance, yet every age change brings new challenges to the unity and cohesion of the family. Likewise, in the Body of Christ, new chapters are always just around the corner and the makeup of the body is constantly changing. Each time, the same core relational lessons must be relearned and applied anew. Absence of conflict isn't the goal, but rather the mind of Christ and a mutual recognition of our continual need for grace.

The dance of unity is *so* worth the effort!

If unity isn't an end in itself but a means to a greater end, it has to be visible to those outside the Body of Christ. This only happens when we're clear on our primary purpose as the Church. The next chapter addresses that clarity, provides a strategy for achieving it, and reveals the stunning results we've already experienced.

QUESTIONS FOR SELF-REFLECTION

- Were you aware of the emphasis the New Testament places on unity/harmony? If not, what does that awareness change for you?

- Which of the wedding vow comparisons most caught your attention?

- What are your thoughts on the very common phenomenon in most cities of church-hopping, people regularly moving from congregation to congregation?

- Do you need to seek reconciliation with someone? Is there someone that God might use you to help reconcile with someone else through prayer and possibly direct intervention?

TODAY'S GPS

Jesus, author of love, we praise and glorify You for the sacrificial and endless agape love that You are, and that You pour out on us. Your commitment to us took You all the way to the cross, and none of our harmful betrayals cause You to reach the end of the line with us. Protect us from the enemy who tries to convince us that broken fellowship is inconsequential, and who seeks to prevent wounds from being healed or forgiven. Sanctify us and purify us from our pride that so quickly sees the blind spots in others and so rarely sees our own. Bless us with the depth of relationship that can only come by working through conflict, and make us peacemakers for one another. Amen.

Chapter Six

VISIBLE UNITY: UNITY AS A MEANS TO AN END

IF maintaining clarity of vision was easy, organizational optometry wouldn't be a cottage industry. Pastors wouldn't receive invitations to conferences on visionary leadership virtually every week. Leaders wouldn't write book after book about vision, and speakers wouldn't be able to fund their children's college education by addressing it. "Keeping the main thing the main thing" is one of the most vital and never-ending aspects of leadership. The first challenge is to determine what the "main thing" is!

At the 2006 Willow Creek Global Leadership Summit, Bill Hybels asked the attendees, "Are you clear on the primary purpose of the Church?" To be honest, I remember my immediate reaction: I wasn't even clear that was a good question. If seminary had required me to wrestle with the question (I don't think it did), I conveniently stored the conclusion alongside the textbooks gathering dust on the shelf. Several possible "primary purposes" immediately coursed through my mind, but I wasn't convinced one should be declared "primary" over the rest.

That question ended up being the zenith of a season of divine discontent, first for me in terms of the primary purpose for the Church, and then for my congregation as it was foisted upon them by me. Divine discontent, a phrase possibly first coined by Ralph Waldo Emerson, aptly applies to chapters in life where God makes a person uncomfortable enough with their present circumstances to then be willing to make necessary changes. By then, I'd been the solo pastor of the congregation for 15 years, and I knew it would've been easier to change the captain than steer the ship in a new direction. I had to be convinced biblically that a course correction was needed if I was going to embark on the process of change, knowing the conflict that was going to inevitably ensue.

I'm no lover of conflict, but I took hold of the wheel. Here are the conclusions I reached from my own biblical study of Hybels' question that gave me the laser focus I needed to redirect our congregation. Knowing what God says about the Church has also increased my conviction in my current capacity of working to see John 17 answered for the Church in my city. The primary purpose of the Church, which was Hybels question, provides clearer vision and direction for each part of the Church in every locale.

THE PRIMARY PURPOSE OF THE CHURCH IS TO GO!

1. *An acceptable question.* Since *my* initial reaction to the challenge was to challenge the question, perhaps I'm not alone. First Corinthians 14:8 says, "If the trumpet does not sound a clear call, who will get ready for battle?" If there *is* a primary purpose of the church, I'd better be clear on it, especially as a leader. Just because the question was new to me wasn't a good reason to ignore it, nor was embarrassment over a seemingly obvious question that I'd never considered.

2. *Jesus' last words.* The last thing someone tells you is what they are particularly convinced you should remember and act upon. Coaches don't pull out the whole playbook during a timeout with the game on the line. They focus on the one strategy that

will create the most positive outcome. Jesus' last words were more consistent than I realized.

- The Great Commission in Matthew is familiar to most Christ followers and is the obvious first place to consider when addressing the primary purpose question. "Then Jesus came to them and said, 'All authority in heaven and on earth has been given to me. [19]Therefore go and make disciples of all nations, baptizing them in the name of the Father and of the Son and of the Holy Spirit, [20]and teaching them to obey everything I have commanded you. And surely I am with you always, to the very end of the age.'" (Matthew 28:18–20)

- Mark's final words of Jesus can be missed because of the manuscript variants in terms of where the gospel originally ended. Some Bibles put the end of Mark 16 in footnotes, making it easier to overlook. If we receive all of it as God's Word, regardless of which biblical authors penned which parts when, then Mark's gospel recalls the same final sentiment as Matthew's. "He (Jesus) said to them, 'Go into all the world and preach the gospel to all creation.'" (Mark 16:15)

- Luke is the author not only of the Gospel but of the sequel, Acts. Jesus' clearest final words show up in Acts, not in Luke. Acts 1:8 adds some details, but the content of Jesus' command is the same. "But you will receive power when the Holy Spirit comes on you; and you will be my witnesses in Jerusalem, and in all Judea and Samaria, and to the ends of the earth." (Acts 1:8)

- Since John doesn't record any pre-ascension words of Jesus, those who do are unanimous.

3. *Jesus' other words.* Jesus taught plenty of things, but on at least two other occasions He directly spoke about His own primary purpose, and echoed what He told His disciples prior to His ascension.

- "For the Son of Man came to seek and to save the lost." (Luke 19:10)

- Jesus replied, "Let us go somewhere else—to the nearby villages—so I can preach there also. That is why I have come." (Mark 1:38)

4. *Examining the alternatives.* When I first heard Hybels pose the question, several highly important purposes of the Church came to mind. I couldn't immediately say that one was primary and the others secondary. The Great Commission was obviously in the running for primary purpose, but only after examining the alternatives did I become thoroughly convinced.

- *Great Commandment* (Matthew 22:37–40). The Great Commandment Jesus taught in the Scriptures is one command-ment with two sides to it: 1) love the Lord your God with all of your heart, soul, strength and mind, and 2) love your neighbor as yourself. If the first part is separated from the second part, it could easily be assumed that the primary purpose of the Church is simply to worship God and to keep growing in our capacity to do so wholeheartedly, single-mind-edly, and all-inclusively. The context of the conversation in Luke 10:25–37, though, is quite revealing and eliminates that narrow interpretation. A man asked Jesus what he must do to inherit eternal life, and He gave the two-sided response followed by the parable of the Great Samaritan which vividly illustrated the "love your neighbor as yourself" teaching. To truly worship and love God means to look outward and love others, too. In the parable, the two who thought they were worshiping God but ignored the person in need were wrong.

- *Love one another* (John 13:34–35; 17:21). Jesus commanded His disciples to love one another so that the world may know that they are His disciples. When Jesus prayed that His followers be perfectly unified, it was so that the world comes to believe. "Love one another" isn't the end, but the means to the end.

- *Abide in Christ* (John 15:5). What if the primary purpose of the Church is simply to abide in Christ—to dwell in Him? That's not a bad possibility, but Jesus said that anyone who does abide in him bears much fruit. While some fruit is internal (such as the fruit of the Holy Spirit), Jesus clearly expects external or outward fruit as well, as indicated by multiple scenes in the Gospels.

- *Be filled with the Holy Spirit* (Luke 24:49, and echoed in Acts 1:8). Maybe it's the end of Luke, where Jesus told the disciples to wait for the Holy Spirit before going out and messing things up by operating out of their own power, that should be seen as our

THE BEST WAY TO PREACH AND MODEL AN UNCONDITIONAL GOSPEL IS UNCONDITIONALLY, LEAVING THE RESULTS TO GOD.

primary purpose—to be filled with the Holy Spirit. I don't argue against that need. But the one completely consistent mark in the book of Acts of being filled with the Holy Spirit is a new courage and success in proclaiming Jesus to others.[1] Being filled with the Spirit is the mechanism by which Jesus' message is proclaimed, but not the primary purpose.

- *Follow Jesus* (whose primary identity is shown in John 1:14). The one that clinched it for me was to simply consider what it means for the Church to follow Jesus, to be the Body of Christ. There's never been a more outward-focused person than Jesus. The whole incarnation is the story of Jesus living for others. He left *Heaven* to come to us. If we're to follow

---

1   I read through every instance in the Book of Acts where it says someone was filled with the Holy Spirit, and while many results differ, successfully proclaiming Jesus to others is the constant.

Him, we're to do the same—leaving behind the spiritually "safe" places and going into the messy world.

All the alternatives, upon further examination, point in the same direction to a single primary purpose.

THE PRIMARY PURPOSE REVEALED

After my biblical examination of Hybels' question, I concluded that the primary purpose of the Church is to *Go*.[2] That kind of simple clarity was new for me, and was incredibly motivating as our congregation navigated through turbulent waters in changing from an inward to an outward focus. The Church is intended to live for others, not ourselves. As Tucson Pastor Virgil Stokes likes to say, "Go is two-thirds of God's name!" An outward focus is essential to being the Church. If we aren't outward focused, we aren't the Church, but something else altogether, perhaps a social club of people filled with similar interests.

HOW THE LOCAL CONGREGATION IS TO GO!

When beginning the process of leading our congregation to more of an outward focus, the biggest argument I encountered centered around the earlier content of this book from Chapters 1 and 2. "Pastor," I heard from many, "we aren't healthy enough to focus on those outside of our fellowship. We need to get better at loving one another internally. We have so many areas where we need to grow and mature within our own congregation. Once we accomplish *those* things, *that's* the time to devote more resources to those outside our walls." My response? When has health ever followed disobedience? If Jesus is clear that we need to Go, then we need to Go. As my wife learned in a parenting class from Barb Tompkins, "Delayed obedience is not obedience."[3]

---

2   For the Greek scholars, I'm fully aware that "go" isn't the primary verb in verse 19, but rather it's "make disciples." Literally, it says, "(In your) going, make disciples..." The going is assumed. For me, that doesn't change the argument, but actually adds to it.

3   Barb Tompkins taught a very popular Mom's Class as part of a John 17 effort for decades in the city, called CARE Women's Bible Study, an acronym for Christ's Arms Reaching Everyone. Women from dozens of churches participated together.

As we've seen repeatedly, the unity Jesus prayed for is a visible unity, not an internal one. If our unity is how the world is supposed to come to know the love of God, our unity can't be contained in the four walls of the church, literally or in terms of the congregations' programs and projects. Neither can we afford to wait until we "get our own house in order" before pursuing unity, since blessing never follows disobedience. Unity/harmony is part of how our own house will mature.

Dan Almeter says, "Our faith isn't a mature faith until it impacts the community." While the quote is noteworthy, Dan's context makes it even more remarkable. He is part of the Alleluia Community in Augusta, Georgia, a covenant community similar to the one described at the end of Acts 2 that's been in existence since the 1970s. People from 12 different denominations own a city block together in one of the most crime-ridden neighborhoods of the city, transforming it through their common and visible unity. For over 35 years, 24-7-365 continuous prayer has been happening in that neighborhood. As a result, other similar "visible unity" communities have been formed around the city and the country *at the request of government leaders!*

Our experience has been stunningly similar in Tucson. If you had asked me in 2011, even after I had become the Church Domain Director in this new 4Tucson adventure, to plot out the path where we'd be five years later, I wouldn't have had the faith to do it. Not in my wildest dreams could I imagine that the Christian community in the sixth least churched city in the country would've gone from invisible (or actively shunned) by city leaders to a widely sought-after partner. How has visible unity/harmony manifested itself in my city so that its people are coming to know the love of God? Take a look at these "new normals" that characterize Tucson.

THE NEW NORMAL IN PUBLIC SCHOOLS

How many times have you heard someone lament, "We kicked God out of the schools fifty years ago?" Public schools have been at the forefront of the culture's assault on Christianity, and the news is still littered with stories of school districts banning mention of Christmas, students reprimanded for quoting the Bible in an assignment, and other forms of hypocritical censorship under the guise of inclusiveness. Few argue that public schools in the United States have improved in these last five decades. Yet individual congregations have for years seen the plight of our public schools as an opportunity to come alongside and offer assistance. The congregation I led partnered with our three neighboring public elementary schools beginning in the mid 1990s, helping students and families at Thanksgiving, Christmas, and other times as needed. At one point, we got a phone call *from* the school asking us if we'd consider starting a Good News Club (from Child Evangelism Fellowship)—an after school club for kids that shares the gospel from the Bible! It's entirely legal for churches to use public space that our tax dollars have paid for; if the school allows any outside group to use its facilities, it can't discriminate on the basis of religion. Local congregations assisting their neighborhood schools isn't a new idea.

> WE'VE HEARD HOW YOUR CHURCHES HAVE ADOPTED SCHOOLS. WOULD YOU CONSIDER ADOPTING US AND OUR STAFF, TOO?

When a congregation is clear on its primary purpose to Go and equip its people to Go, starting with a neighboring school can be incredibly strategic. The school touches the entire fabric of the neighborhood: children, parents, grandparents, aunts and uncles; employees in various businesses; members of neighborhood associations; and all of the ethnic groups of the neighborhood. Plus, the variety of different ways a school can be served match the varied interests in the congregation—from cooking to cleaning, tutoring to mentoring, repair projects, and so forth.[4] When what's happening on the local, individual level gets intentionally linked with Jesus' John 17 prayer, the impact explodes!

---

4   4Tucson created a document called "101 Ways and More Your Church Can Partner With A Public School" to illustrate ways that everyone in the congregation can get engaged with a local school.

Matt Merrill, a gifted local Christian leader in his mid-twenties, was the city leader of an "Eleven-11" prayer movement, so named for its goal of renting out 11 schools throughout our state for 26-hour prayer vigils culminating on 11/11/11, November 11, 2011. Churches from the community came together to lead times of worship, and students and faculty from the schools were invited as well. Amazing stories of transformation resulted among attendees, from suicidal individuals changing their minds to teachers and administrators who saw the entire culture of their school change. Christians who participated in the vigils went from prayer to acts of service because prayer had reoriented their hearts and minds to see what God sees.

The intentionality to serve schools took two forms. Individual congregations around the city regularly approached area schools more often asking how they could help, with 4Tucson Education Domain Director Bernadette Gruber providing training on how to do this legally and effectively. The training emphasizes, "Our goal is to make teachers' and administrators' jobs easier and better, not more complicated and painful. Unnecessarily putting people in hot water helps nobody." Simultaneously, citywide Christian leaders met with superintendents of the city's public school districts, asking, "As Christians and community members in your district, how can we pray for you and how can we help?" Once they saw that we meant *exactly that* and not, "How can we lobby, complain, or seek reciprocity?" doors *flung* open. Kristine Sommer from Southlake Church in Portland, Oregon, another city where such partnerships have taken hold, says in their video, *Undivided,* "The best way to convince schools you don't have an agenda is to not have an agenda." At 4Tucson, we tell leaders all the time that the best way to preach and model an unconditional gospel is unconditionally, leaving the results to God.

Founder and President of Gateway to Better Education, Eric Buehrer, says, "Schools have turned from battlegrounds to beautiful gardens." By uniting/harmonizing according to every principle discussed in the first five chapters of this book, 80 percent of the public schools in our city were in partnership with a local congregation by fall 2016. Five area school districts regularly hold appreciation events thanking pastors for their partnership and sharing ways those partnerships can grow. Christian leaders are regularly invited to be part of district and school policy and hiring teams. At our one-day Pastor Prayer Summit on November 3, 2016, we shared this good news, and the immediate response was to begin praying that *every* public school in Tucson have a church partner by the same time the following year. Individuals who were at first skeptical if not outright hostile toward the partnerships have become their biggest advocates: a principal who resisted the idea of a church meeting on his campus is now a member of that congregation; a teacher who shared the buzz in the teacher's lounge about "what does this church *really* want" decided to check it out for himself and joined the congregation; an initially unconvinced administrator has moved to a new city and started church-school partnerships there. I've preached Matthew 5:13–16, where Jesus declares us to be salt and light, for 30 years, but I've never seen anything like this!

THE NEW NORMAL IN FOSTER CARE

4Tucson got a call one day from the Pauline Machiche, the Pima County Program Administrator of the Department of Child Safety, or Child Protective Services as it had been known previously. She said, "We've heard how your churches have adopted schools. Would you consider adopting us and our staff, too? Because we're hurting and the government alone can't fix it."

At our next three-day Pastor Prayer Summit, we prayed over this incredible invitation, and two pastors stepped forward to explore the possibilities further. One of those pastors has since become 4Tucson Social Services Domain Director J. Michael Davis. As the neutral player in the city (we don't represent any single denomination, ethnicity, church size, non-profit, etc.), we had already been given the opportunity to host a citywide "Our Kids, Our Care" event bringing together different Christian organizations working in the foster care and group home arenas. Competition in our city is giving way to, "How can we do this together?" which, if you know anything about Tucson's history, was until recent years an absolutely foreign question.

A Department of Child Safety-church partnership team was formed, and some congregations adopted the various agencies around the city, providing prayer, meals, and other support. We learned of a program called CarePortal out of the Global Orphan Project in Kansas City, MO, where child welfare workers discover needs in the families they're working with, and then enter those needs into a software program that sends the requests to congregations who've signed up as partners. Those congregations commit to pray for, and if they can, meet the needs. There's even a GPS component to the software so that when enough congregations are engaged, the request goes to the congregation(s) closest to the family in need.

> THE CHURCH IS ON THE RADAR OF ALL TUCSON CITY LEADERS, AND FOR THE FIRST TIME IN ANYONE'S MEMORY, IT'S POSITIVE!

CarePortal was developing an ability to franchise and launch in other cities. Because we were already working on citywide visible unity/harmony, and the government had requested help from the faith community, Tucson became an ideal pilot for CarePortal in the western U.S. The program launched in Pima County in December 2015—and brace yourself for these statistics from the one year anniversary, shared by CarePortal Regional Manager Sue Baird:

In one year...
- 816 children from 324 families impacted.
- 27 churches actively involved, with another five waiting.
- 402 agency reviews from DCS workers, which are 100 percent positive!
- 98 percent positive rating from the churches involved.
- The numbers of children entering foster care in our county dropped by over six percent, reversing a lengthy trend.

- The Arizona governor came to Tucson to share, "This is how child welfare was intended to happen because the State makes a terrible parent." He further announced his intention to take the program statewide.

THE NEW NORMAL IN COLLABORATION

The 4Tucson Church Domain launched a new program in 2017 called Pastors' Edge, where senior/solo pastors come together monthly to do two things: learn best practices from each other and meet in small groups determined by geographic location to develop deep relationships and pray for one another. A new-to-Tucson pastor exclaimed after the second meeting, "This is incredible. I've seen other places where this happens within a denomination or network, but crossing denominations and ethnicities? What an amazing gift you have here."

When about a dozen of our Pastors Partnership went together to see a matinee of *42* (The story of baseball great Jackie Robinson), the looks we got when we all walked in together were priceless. The stares and eavesdropping from those in the lobby and restaurant afterwards as we discussed and processed the movie together were even better.

Church planting, or launching new congregations, has been an inherently competitive enterprise. As the country has grown more secular,[5] existing congregations have become less threatened by new church plants, recognizing that there's no shortage of "customers." Yet even networks and organizations that promote church planting tend to develop their own tools and resources and can easily fall into a competitive mindset. Bucking that trend, 4Tucson recently appointed Becki Kern as the new Church Planting Resource Coordinator. Becki had already been networking in the church planting arena as the Campus Launch Pastor at Pantano Christian Church. They've planted four churches in Southern Arizona and helped keep another inner city church plant going, partnering with very dissimilar congregations in

---

5   The number of unchurched people in the country nearly doubled from 39,000,000 to 76,000,000 since 2000, according to the Barna Group.

doing so. Under the direction of Lead Pastor Glen Elliott, they recently committed to "never again plant a church by ourselves." Pooling our resources citywide, church planting as a whole City Church will be much more effective and closer to the heart of Jesus' John 17 prayer.

Speaking of competition, public school districts literally compete with one another (as well as charter and private schools) for state tax dollars that are based on their enrollment. With open enrollment and a very active charter school program, the environment in Tucson is not exactly conducive to collaboration. In 2013, 4Tucson first partnered with the Global Leadership Summit to make the Summit available to leaders at half the price if they were partnered with 4Tucson. Thanks to the generosity of the Willow Creek Association, we've continued that partnership every year since, more than doubling the number of people participating in our city. We held lunches the first day of the 2013 Summit based on the common interests (domains) of leaders, such as Church, Education, Government, Business, and so on. At the Education Domain breakout session, leaders from five different school districts were present, and because of the environment, they started collaborating, sharing resources, and learning from one another. Today, leaders from seven different public school districts meet quarterly with 4Tucson Education Domain Director Bernadette Gruber to continue this collaboration.

4Tucson Government Domain Director Paul Parisi hosts an annual blessing event where Christian leaders gather around elected officials from both political parties and fulfill our biblical responsibility to pray for those in positions of authority. At the January 2017 event, Tucson Mayor Jonathan Rothschild approached me afterward with an idea and a question. He wanted to emphasize the need for mentoring in our city, particularly for what he called youth of color who were on waiting lists. He said, "I think the Church could be a great source for mentors, but I could use help bringing together the African American and Hispanic pastors in the community to assist with this mission. Do you think you could help?" I didn't have to think long about that question! When we met for lunch the next month, I brought along one of the most well-connected pastors from each group and we had a wonderful time together. Rothschild is Jewish and had told the mentoring organizations about his upcoming lunch with us. Their comment back to him was, "That's exactly the right move, because the faith-based community is the one who can deliver."

These aren't the only examples, but just some of the most compelling to date at a citywide level. The Church is on the radar of all Tucson city leaders, and for the first time in anyone's memory, it's positive! Do you think Jesus knew what He was doing when He went to His knees? I do! I can't even conceive of a more successful strategy than the one He prayed for and outlined in John 17.

OPERATIONALIZING JESUS' STRATEGY

> SPLITTING LIFE INTO SACRED AND SECULAR SIMPLY MUST STOP.

4Tucson's Tony Simms, has a favorite word: operationalize. "How are we going to operationalize this?" he asks regularly as his way of saying, "How are we going to make this happen?" As has been oft-cited, the road to hell is paved with good intentions.[6] Visible unity/harmony is a great concept, flowing straight out of Jesus' primary purpose for the Church, but how are we going to "operationalize" it? How will we ensure that it happens rather than remain a concept to be cheered along from a distance, a great intention that nobody's intentional about? Unity/harmony in smaller units, like congregations, is a fine beginning, but not large enough for the world to notice.

In *Jesus' Surprising Strategy*, I devoted the final two chapters to laying out how 4Tucson is structured. Over these last six years, we've learned about many different communities that are paying attention to Jesus' John 17 prayer for visible unity/harmony. The structure and leadership differ greatly from city to city, but the call of God is similar. Most cities

---

6   John Ray, in 1670, cited as a proverb "Hell is paved with good intentions." Even earlier than that, it's been attributed to Saint Bernard of Clairvaux (1091–1153), as "Hell is full of good intentions or desires."

we've encountered are working out of a domain wheel concept of some form or another. Here's ours:

Jesus isn't just praying that Christians unite in the Church and Prayer Domains. He's praying that our unity/harmony enable us to function as salt and light in every domain of society. All the way back to the first chapter of the Bible, in God's first spoken word to His newly created humans, God gave us the responsibility to have dominion over the Earth (Genesis 1:28). "Domains" operationalize that command. Unity isn't the end, it's the means to the end; the end is that the city be transformed and bring glory to God, which also enables every person in the city to experience the life Jesus came to make possible, an abundant life lived to the full (John 10:10).

SACRED/SECULAR SEGREGATION

A massive roadblock to God's intentions is that our culture likes to compartmentalize. Men are typically quite proficient at this ability. Bill and Pam Farrel wrote *Men Are Like Waffles—Women Are Like Spaghetti* back in 2001, creating a powerful word picture from the observation that men usually work in boxes while women connect the dots. Conversations in my marriage often end up looking like a waffle/spaghetti wrestling match.

While women compartmentalize less than men, there are areas where gender seems to have little impact on who boards the waffle express.

One of the most destructive examples of this tendency is the segregation of life into sacred and secular compartments. This disease traces back to the time of Jesus when Gnostic dualism was rampant and eventually deemed heretical, contradicting the truth of the gospel. In the first century, sacred/secular dualism commonly manifested with the spiritual realm seen as good and the natural realm bad. Jesus' incarnation was deemed impossible since He merged the two in leaving Heaven to take on flesh on Earth.[7]

Fast forward to today, and sacred/secular dualism litters our language. We "go to church" even though the word "church" literally is *ecclesia*, or the called-out ones, meaning a people. We can't *go* to church; we *are* the Church. We take *the church* with us wherever we go. The Church goes rather than we go to church. The argument that the culture kicked God out of the schools fifty years ago is dualistic in nature. As long as there are Christians in public schools, God hasn't been entirely removed—and of course, the long-standing joke is that as long as there are tests, there will be prayer in schools. Whether the U.S. Supreme Court decision on prayer was helpful or not is a different and multi-faceted conversation. For Christians to refer to that decision and others like it as justification for forming monasteries isolated from the world, though, is indefensible. It's in direct disobedience to Jesus' commission to us.

Far from being an exercise in semantics, the efforts to segregate sacred and secular are perhaps the biggest contributor to the degradation of culture. Salt in Jesus' day was a preservative: remove the salt and things spoil. Lest we blame the culture, the courts, or some other "secular" entity for this (forgetting, of course, that in our system of government we get who we elect), the desire to separate the two is thoroughly embraced by the Church. Missional author and speaker Reggie McNeal has often stated that instead of the Church being the salt of the Earth, we've functioned like a desalination plant, sucking the salt out of the community and into the church. If we aren't thrilled about the spoiling of the culture, we're reaping what we've sown. When we do church-school partnership trainings, we often have to show teachers

---

7   See *Surprised by Hope*, by N.T. Wright, for further reading on this topic.

and administrators in the schools that it's legal, and leaders and attendees of the churches that it's desirable.

Common understanding is that the sacred parts of our lives include activities such as our church activities, worship, prayer, and daily devotions, while the secular parts are everything else. The heretical but most commonly operationalized belief is that once you've checked off your religious box for the day, you get to be lord of the rest of it. A domain approach to Christianity attempts to recognize and break down this silo mentality, understanding that for a city to be changed, transformation and revival need to take place in every domain, not just the institutional church or "sacred silo."

MISSION BECOMES EVERY CHRIST FOLLOWER'S AGENDA EVERY DAY.

Other examples of dualism include how many congregations and most Christians limit the words "mission" or "ministry" to "churchy" things. The high-water mark for mission for a chosen few churchgoers is to save up for years to participate in a short-term mission trip, after which secular life returns. We "call" church employees but "hire" everyone else; college students who come to take their faith seriously abandon their preparations for "secular" employment to devote their lives to "ministry." I remember well the day a faithful devoted Christ follower who was also a highly-trained kidney specialist and professor came to me to apologize that she didn't have more time for "ministry," meaning ushering, teaching Sunday School, or anything else that could show up in a church bulletin. Caring for hurting people and training others to do the same as a Christ follower isn't ministry?

Instead of mission seen as the exception, we need to come to a place where mission is the norm. Teachers are missionaries to their schools. Business people are missionaries to their colleagues and customers. Medical professionals are missionaries to their patients—and on and on, in every domain. Just like traveling to Tanzania, missionaries need to learn about their contexts, what's appropriate and helpful and what isn't.

Sometimes we evangelize in words, but we always evangelize in actions. We can learn plenty from foreign mission experiences about how to do missions in everyday life, and we must—so that mission becomes every Christ follower's agenda every day.

John O'Hair, a former missionary for 14 years in Kenya, has served 22 years as the headmaster at one of the Christian schools in Tucson. He hammers away at sacred/secular dualism every opportunity he gets. In a sermon at my family's home congregation, he summarized the entire Bible in this regard in three simple sentences. 1) In the Garden of Eden in Genesis, the Kingdom of God and the kingdom of the world were one and the same. 2) Christmas restores the connection; Jesus is Lord of Heaven and Earth. 3) Revelation announces the eternal fusion. Jesus' most famous prayer isn't John 17, but what we've come to term The Lord's Prayer, and in it we pray, "Thy kingdom come, thy will be done, on Earth as it is in Heaven." Splitting life into sacred and secular simply must stop.

Lest there be confusion, the Bible does make a distinction between darkness and light, between the Kingdom of God and kingdom of the world. Blending the two or ignoring the distinction is not the solution. The argument is that when we try to compartmentalize the world into sacred and secular, we do exactly what Jesus told us *not* to do—hide our lights under spiritual containers (Matthew 5:15–16).

Developing a Cross culture—unity/harmony that transcends a homogenous ethnicity—can prove helpful here, too. Some of the Barna Group's most recent research directly reveals how our isolation has led to our immaturity, particularly where sacred/secular segregation is concerned.

> Black communities tend toward communal rhythms of
> spiritual development while white communities prefer
> a more individualistic setting. It is unsurprising there-
> fore that white Christians are more likely to view their
> spiritual life as "entirely private" (42 percent compared

to 32 percent). Black Christians, on the other hand, are much more likely to believe their personal spiritual life has an impact on others—whether they are relatives, friends, community, or society at large. For instance, black Christians are much more likely to believe that their personal spiritual lives have an impact on broader society (46 percent compared to 27 percent)...This was a strong belief of Martin Luther King, and it appears to have had great staying power. He fundamentally believed that one's personal spiritual life had implications for societal justice, and he called Christians—on both sides of the debate—to bring their faith to bear on the struggle for civil rights, to which he dedicated his life. This impact is also tied to the approach to evangelism: half of black Christians (50 percent compared to 34 percent) believe it is their responsibility to tell others about their religious beliefs, further reinforcing the public/private contrast between both groups.[8]

> EVERYONE BENEFITS WITH ALIGNMENT TO HIS PRINCIPLES BECAUSE GOD IS FOR US, NOT AGAINST US.

FROM DOMAINS TO TASKFORCES

Even if we could arrive at a place where everyone understood themselves to be full-time missionaries for Christ (with only the mission settings differing), I don't think that automatically translates into the full extent of what Jesus was praying. Sacred/secular dualism is so ingrained in the culture that residue lasts even after we've shot the concept down.

Unsurprisingly, many understand their missionary tasks in their "secular" settings to be witnessing about Jesus in actions until words

---

8   Barna, "Racial Divides in Spiritual Practice," *Research Releases in Culture and Media*, January 12, 2017.

become possible and appropriate. That's certainly part of the Great Commission. But I don't think it comes very close to the salt and light that Jesus referred to, or the "dominion" found in God's first instruction to humanity. City transformation, as 4Tucson's Founder and Executive Director Mark Harris defines it, is bringing all of the city's structures and institutions into alignment with biblical principles. Salt both preserves and keeps things from spoiling, but it also brings out the full natural flavor of whatever it touches. Everyone benefits with alignment to His principles because God is for us, not against us.

Is the mark of a Christian disciple arriving at a place where he or she can truly say that Jesus has first place—that He is more important than anything else life has to offer? I don't think so. I think dualism has infiltrated once again when we think that way. As mentioned previously, Jesus doesn't want to be at the top of my list; He wants to be the list! His goal isn't to see the spiritual compartment grow bigger than any of the rest. He wants to be Lord not just of my spiritual compartments but of *all* of my compartments. He wants to be Lord of my marriage, Lord of my family, Lord of my employment, Lord of my entertainment and recreation—Lord of all. *Everything* in life that is subject to the lordship of Christ is better than *anything* in life that isn't.

Going into 2017, 4Tucson has intentionally started working on the next stage of our strategy—moving from domains to taskforces. Domains bring together Christ followers in each area of the culture. Taskforces bring together *all* of the domains to tackle an issue. Through research of city and county documents, 4Tucson has identified 22 focus areas in our city that will all need to be addressed for our city to truly thrive the way God intends. If these problems were easy to solve, someone would have done so long ago! Our city's issue isn't that we've lacked smart people. Our city's issue is that we've lacked visible unity/harmony.

The first focus area we're tackling is called Poverty Reduction. Tucson consistently ranks in the top 10 most impoverished cities in the country. Many people have just accepted this as our lot in life: time and again we hear leaders say, "Tucson has always been a low wage town, and always will be." Who says? We know poverty will never be eliminated, for many reasons straight out of the Bible. But it can certainly be dramatically reduced.

Each domain brings its own perspective to the issues of poverty. The Business Domain points to the need for employment; the Social Services Domain addresses barriers to employment; the Healthcare Domain focuses on physical and mental health needs; the Education Domain emphasizes the importance of education and training, and so forth. Can any of these *alone* significantly and systemically reduce poverty? No. The Government Domain has a role to play, but government was never intended to function independently from the other domains.

OUR CITY'S ISSUE ISN'T THAT WE'VE LACKED SMART PEOPLE. OUR CITY'S ISSUE IS THAT WE'VE LACKED VISIBLE UNITY/HARMONY.

The result of the taskforce's research was shockingly uncomplicated. If three conditions are met, a person has less than a three percent chance of landing in poverty: graduate from high school, secure employment, and wait to have children until marriage. All of the domains can work together to operationalize those three conditions, and if they do, 98 percent of any city's residents will be out of poverty.

I'm convinced that one of the most strategic ways in which Christians can be salty and flavor and preserve the culture is by modeling what true unity/harmony looks like. It's not uniformity: biblical unity is neither each part identical and emphasizing the same things, nor is it all of the parts blended together until none excel at anything. When we truly understand that we don't live for ourselves or die for ourselves (Romans 14:8), our approach to life completely changes. Focusing on a common Lord helped our Pastors Partnership bridge the political divide. If enough Christians flavor the conversation in tackling a common issue like Poverty Reduction from each of their domain's perspectives, yet being subject to one another and one another's viewpoints out of reverence for Christ (Ephesians 5:21), I believe Jesus will be glorified, the enemy blocked, the participants sanctified, and solutions found.

IT'S MORE BIBLICAL THAN WE THOUGHT

Faith and belief in Jesus mean more than trusting Jesus with the right answers on religion tests. The Romans Road (verses out of the book of Romans that help lead a person to accepting Jesus as Savior and going to Heaven upon death) is built on the foundation of the Old Testament prophets, who regularly expressed a concern for justice and alignment *in this life*. Eternal life doesn't begin when we die; it begins when we enter into a saving relationship with Jesus.

We're more comfortable *listening* to Handel's *Messiah* than we are contemplating it. "The kingdom of the world has become the kingdom of our Lord" is taken straight from Revelation 11:15. We're more comfortable reciting the Lord's Prayer (Matthew 6:9–13) than working to answer it. References to the city are all through the Bible, which starts in a garden (Eden) and ends in a city (the new Jerusalem.)[9] The concept that all of life is to be subject to our Lord is thoroughly biblical.

The book of Nehemiah has been powerfully used for training in the leadership principles that Nehemiah employs. The rebuilt wall around Jerusalem can also be seen allegorically as the spiritual wall of protection that our families and cities need. What I found interesting as I recently read again through Nehemiah is the number of different domains specifically mentioned as working together to rebuild the wall. About half of our 12 domains in 4Tucson are cited in Nehemiah 3. Furthermore, Nehemiah called for each family to build and protect their part of the wall while also calling for help from everyone else when their section was attacked.

In 2017, 4Tucson began training on what it truly means to go about the work of city transformation. One of the first sessions by Tony

---

9   Note Psalm 132:15, Isaiah 62:4, 12, Isaiah 64:10, and Hebrews 11:10, 16.

Simms so powerfully illuminated the biblical basis, not only for the work we're doing but the processes we've undertaken, that I've included it as Appendix 2.

Visible unity/harmony in Tucson, like the spiritual wall of protection around a city, is far from complete. When I read the book of Nehemiah, I'm stunned at how quickly the wall came together. Likewise, when I look at what's been accomplished with visible unity/harmony in Tucson, I'm shocked at how much progress has been made with so few partners (compared to the potential). In fact, two different visionary comments were recently made within hours of one another from two very different voices in our city. The first was by a phenomenal twenty-something Christian leader, Zach Yentzer. He recently married and bought a home near downtown to intentionally align with Jeremiah 29. Tucson's downtown revitalization project known as Rio Nuevo was a bad joke for decades, marred by mismanagement and waste. But now a "new river" (in Spanish, *rio nuevo*) is truly flowing, and Zach is part of a group of people working on revitalization so that downtown Tucson is truly a blessing for all its residents, not just a few. He said, "I'm praying that Tucson becomes the Silicon Valley for faith engaged in the culture—a proving ground, a laboratory." Check out his project, 100 Creative Cities, at www.100creativecities. com as it works to bring the generations together for creative problem solving. That same day, 4Tucson's Mark Harris met with a staff member from the state governor's office to give him the research report produced by the Poverty Reduction taskforce. How incredibly motivating it was to communicate that we don't have to focus on hundreds of problems to reduce poverty, but only three. As the conversation drew to a close, Mark suggested to him that he might want to buy real estate in Tucson because "in five years, this will be the place to be."

> THE REBUILT WALL AROUND JERUSALEM CAN ALSO BE SEEN ALLEGORICALLY AS THE SPIRITUAL WALL OF PROTECTION THAT OUR FAMILIES AND CITIES NEED.

Whether Tucson ever becomes the Silicon Valley of faith engaging the culture or not, and whether Tucson's real estate market and economy are the envy of the state in five years or not, I don't know. I *do* know that both sound like praying the way Jesus taught: that the Kingdom of God come and God's will be done, right here in our city. Both are pictures of visible unity/harmony with Christians working together in every domain of the culture to create a city being transformed and blessed, all to the glory of God.

———

Should we spend more time praying or more time working? Is transformation God's job or ours? Should we wait on God or is God waiting on us? God's part/our part is the subject of the next chapter.

QUESTIONS FOR SELF-REFLECTION

- Do you agree that the Church's primary purpose (and therefore the purpose of every part of the Church) is to Go? If not, why not? If so, what needs to change for you to more fully align with that purpose?

- Which of the stories included in this chapter do you find most inspirational? Why?

- Where do you most likely fall into the sacred/secular trap?

- Where in your city is Christian unity/harmony most visible? In which arenas is God calling you to engage?

TODAY'S GPS

Lord Jesus, we bow down together before You, praising Your Holy name as King of kings and Lord of lords, ruler of Heaven and Earth. We acknowledge Your lordship over all, over every compartment and sector and domain and nation. In humble awe and adoration, we praise You for visibly leaving the perfectly safe and peaceful confines of Heaven to join us here in our sinful broken condition on Earth. Protect us from the enemy who seeks to mute our influence by convincing us to only pay attention to "spiritual" things. Protect us from enemy-inspired pride and foolishness that tempt us to judge the world instead of serve our neighbors. Sanctify, purify, and mature us until we attain the whole measure of the fullness of Christ, functioning as Your body in all of the Earth. Amen.

Chapter Seven

LET'S FORM A COMMITTEE AND PART THE RED SEA: GOD'S PART/OUR PART

IF crucifixion was easy—well, that's a sentence that has no appropriate completion. "Crucifixion" and "easy" are like the oil and water comparison on steroids. They don't mix, not for a minute, not in any setting.

During some of the intense challenges of the first half of 2016, I noticed something about a word I used but never fully contemplated: "excruciating" has the cross right in the middle of it.[1] Excruciating is a word we use to describe the most difficult of circumstances, and in terms of etymology, the word came into being because it reflects the most difficult moment in all of human history. Crucifixion is well-documented as one of the most sadistic of all forms of human torture, which given humanity's tortuous history is saying something. To add insult to injury, Jesus' crucifixion came immediately on the heels of a near fatal flogging. Jesus' physical agony and suffering at the crucifixion were incomprehensible. He was mocked by those in charge, tormented by those being crucified beside him, and abandoned by nearly all his friends. The accompanying emotional agony was equally extreme.

---

1 *Crux* is Latin for cross.

But Jesus' physical and emotional suffering on the cross doesn't even register when compared with his *spiritual* suffering. Many others in Jesus' day were tortured and killed via crucifixion; two were crucified right next to Him. But His spiritual suffering stands alone. Jesus experienced perfect unity with the Father and unhindered bliss in Heaven before voluntarily leaving both in the greatest act of *Go*ing ever. He quoted from Psalm 22 on the cross, "My God, my God, why have you forsaken me?" He wasn't embellishing. He wasn't having a low-faith moment. He wasn't merely identifying with other sufferers (like David, whom he quoted) in their excruciating moments. Jesus was articulating an experience He chose on our behalf so that we never need to experience it ourselves. In taking on the cumulative sin inventory of each person who has ever lived, He was *actually* abandoned by God. The spotless Lamb provided the only sacrifice that could sufficiently cover the mound of debt we'd accumulated as a human race. Jesus was forsaken by His Heavenly Father, with whom He'd experienced perfect fellowship for all eternity, in order that we might never have to be forsaken by God. *That's* truly what "excruciating" means.

> WHAT LOOKS LIKE CONFUSION TO US IS STANDARD OPERATING PROCEDURE FOR GOD.

Comparatively, then, my days were closer to Disneyland-ish than excruciating. Nevertheless, what Jesus prayed for immediately *prior* to His excrucation was being challenged in my world daily, with the stakes seeming to rise with every iteration. The devil was throwing everything at us, including the kitchen sink and the cabinet it was in, and some of it was starting to wound us. I wrote this in my journal on February 25, 2016: "I don't think I've ever been so discouraged. I have no clue what direction to proceed. Unity and trust with everyone feels damaged. I feel very alone. Of course, that could just be my depression talking, further disqualifying me on mental health grounds. Or it could be my inability to discern talking, further disqualifying me on spiritual grounds. I feel totally trapped and totally incompetent. I trust *you*, Lord—you're the one who prayed for all this unity stuff. But I don't trust *myself*."

I was heading into a meeting for which I felt completely ill-equipped mentally, emotionally, and spiritually. On the table were some choices with extremely high stakes, including whether or not I was going to continue in my current capacity with 4Tucson. Simultaneously, I was also a few days away from preaching a newer message at a church in Tucson. Often when I'm asked to preach, congregations want to hear a message on John 17 or 1 Corinthians 12, along with encouragement for what God's doing in our city and opportunities for how they can get off the sidelines and into the game. While I always try to contextualize those messages, much of the basic content is the same. My assignment the coming Sunday, though, was to preach the next leg of their series on The Story, a chronological walk through the high points of the entire Bible. My task was to preach on the Exodus.

God had already been showing me with greater and greater clarity the truth of Jesus' statement from John 15:5, "Apart from me you can do nothing." A few weeks earlier, I found myself describing the God's part/our part discussion using the phrase, "Let's form a committee and part the Red Sea." There are some situations so dire that unless God intervenes, there won't be an intervention. So, in God's always perfect timing, I was living out my upcoming sermon theme in far more vivid ways than I preferred. When I checked in with the host pastor early in the week, I explained my situation and the very unknown outcome at that point and admitted, "I may have to simply blubber my way through my journal and call it a sermon. Are you cool with that?" I figured he was going to have to clean up my mess, so he should have the option of changing directions if he wanted. He prayed with me and we continued with the plan to leap off the ledge together that coming Sunday.

My message that morning began, "Have you ever been in a situation where you had the Red Sea on one side, and the Egyptians breathing down your neck on the other side? That's exactly where I've been recently. In talking to Pastor John this last week, I wasn't sure whether to laugh or to cry. If this whole unity deal was easy, Jesus wouldn't have prayed for it. I warned John that by today I might be a wreck, reading my journal and calling it a sermon, but here we are." I looked at my notes, then back up at the congregation. I took a deep breath and exhaled. "Well, I'm happy to report that out of the fires, God has forged an even deeper love than we had before. God delivered, and the Red Sea of conflict has been parted. But frankly, it would have been easier to quit." Then I continued, "Have you ever prayed for God to move in God-sized ways? If you have, you're asking for it! If human solutions will do it, it won't take a miracle. It's like saying, 'Let's form a committee and part the Red Sea.' Jesus said, 'Apart from me you can do nothing.' It takes Red Sea experiences—regularly—to truly believe that."

What does the whole Red Sea committee-that-never-happened story have to do with Jesus' strategy for maturing the church and engaging the world? The previous chapter ended with Jesus teaching us to pray, "Thy kingdom come, thy will be done" in our city, praying into reality the vision from Revelation where the kingdom of the world has become the kingdom of our God. This raises a rather significant theological question: whose responsibility is it to make this happen? It's possible that I could have given the impression earlier that if we humans work hard enough or strategize effectively enough on visible unity/harmony, we will then "operationalize" the Lord's Prayer on our own. Ultimately, *only* God can do this; that's why "thy kingdom come" is a prayer, not an instruction manual. It is the height of arrogance to think that me, my church, or my citywide organization can have that kind of authority or success. Yet God rarely works without human agents. When He does—when He simply takes the situation into His own hands—we call it a miracle to emphasize its abnormality. The phrase "Body of Christ" itself points to God's incredible decision to allow us mere sinful humans to play a part in the divine drama. We can align ourselves with God's work or not. We can be part of the solution or remain part of the problem.

Jesus taught His disciples in John 13 to love one another and provided a powerful visual aid for what loving one another looks like by washing the disciples' feet. We have a part to play with servant responsibilities in unity/harmony that are ours to carry out. But later that night He was burdened in prayer on the same topic, beseeching his Heavenly Father to make the disciples one. God also has a part to play with breakthroughs in unity/harmony that only He can provide. How do we know which is which?

That very question was the impetus for writing *Jesus' Surprising Strategy*. Having spent a couple of years working full time to see Jesus' prayer answered in Tucson, I had observed places where unity/harmony tended to break down, as well as learned perspectives that helped work through those barriers. The entire middle section of that book describes levels of unity/harmony, concentric circles that constantly demand our intentionality. I wrote:

> IN THE BEGINNING AND THE END, GOD'S IN CHARGE, BUT IN THE HEAT OF THE BATTLE, WE HAVE A PART TO PLAY IN THE CHOICES WE MAKE.

When we notice another believer's blind spot, we can learn to proceed with grace and truth. When cultural differences start to create friction and misunderstandings, we can ask questions with grace and truth. When another's sin hurts us, we can do what Jesus did when our sin hurt Him—learn to live life filled with grace and truth. We can remember Level 1, common kindness, and ask more while assuming less. We can recall Level 2, and use the truth we share as a common cause to motivate us to work through our differences rather than retreat because of them. We can bring to mind Level 3 and pray for a growing love for one another that is deeper than emotion, but instead represents a decision and commitment to stay together. We can be mindful of Level 4 and come to the cross in humility, recognizing our total dependence on God in this complex relationship enterprise.[2]

---

2   *Jesus' Surprising Strategy*, p. 105.

Yet we can carry out our part of the equation and still land in places of paralysis where, unless God intervenes, breakdown and break up (not breakthrough) will be the outcome. Not only can this happen, I believe God *wills* it to happen. God intends it because it's in those places where faith, trust, and dependence on God grows, and where we learn most powerfully how to partner with God by staying in our lanes and doing what we're called to do.

PARTING THE SEA OF RED: LESSONS FROM EXODUS 13–14

I shared in the last chapter about my congregation's journey toward a more outward focus. A few years into that transition, we had taken several strong steps of faith, sending nine people to Tanzania, changing some staff positions, assisting in the start of two new churches, and building what we hoped would function as a "community center" for our part of town. Then the 2008 recession hit. Many people who had pledged financial support at sacrificial levels lost jobs or significant income. We did what we could as a congregation to tighten our belts, but we were facing a growing sea of red ink. Unless God intervened, we weren't going to make it.

I remember preaching a series in 2009 during Lent, the forty days leading up to Easter. We called it, "Parting the Sea of Red: From Exodus to Easter." We needed a miracle and I knew it was going to have two components: each of us personally trusting God enough to do what He told us to do while simultaneously trusting Him with the bigger financial mountain that we could not scale through our own plotting and scheming. That series focused on the forgotten chapters, Exodus 13–14, between the Passover and the parting of the Red Sea. Here's an adaptation in relation to unity/harmony of what God showed us.

1. *Foresight: God has it, we don't.* Plenty of times in Exodus 1–12, the Israelites' faith must have been tested to the breaking point during 400 years of slavery, a new edict demanding the drowning of the male babies, and a rescuer (Moses) showing up after

40 years of absence whose arrival only made conditions worse. By the time the plagues were completed and Pharaoh and the Egyptians were more than happy to get rid of them, it must have seemed like a fairy tale to the Israelites, complete with the requisite ending, "and they lived happily ever after." Except that's not at all how it went.

What looks like confusion to us is standard operating procedure for God. The path God led them down toward freedom reveals quite effectively God's foresight and our lack of it. Exodus 13:17 said, "When Pharaoh let the people go, God did not lead them on the road through the Philistine country, though that was shorter. For God said, 'If they face war, they might change their minds and return to Egypt.'" Exodus 14:2–3 added, "Tell the Israelites to turn back and encamp near Pi Hahiroth, between Migdol and the sea. They are to encamp by the sea, directly opposite Baal Zephon. ³Pharaoh will think, 'The Israelites are wandering around the land in confusion, hemmed in by the desert.'"

The Bible tells us that God led the Israelites by a pillar of cloud in front and a pillar of fire in the back, which is itself quite revealing. How many of us would choose to be led by clouds instead of light? God's ways truly are not our ways. First Peter 4:12 indeed states, "Dear friends, do not be surprised at the fiery ordeal that has come on you to test you, as though something strange were happening to you." God wants us—needs us—to be at a place where we well understand John 15:5; not only can we do nothing apart from Him, we don't even know where to start and which way to go. He wants us to learn trust and reliance.

2. *Foe: there is one!* When we're up against the Red Sea on one side and the Egyptians hot on our tail on the other, do we need to be reminded that there's an enemy? No—more likely we need to be reminded that there's a God. But when life is at least

relatively smooth, especially here in the materialistic West, we often forget there's an enemy. We forget that there's an eternal battle going on and that Satan constantly seeks to divide and conquer. We will likely handle many of the challenges to unity/ harmony much better if we anticipate their arrival, even if we can't exactly predict what form the challenges will take.

THE DIFFERENCE BETWEEN WALKING IN FEAR AND WALKING IN FAITH IS SOMETIMES AS SIMPLE AS WHO WE TALK TO WHEN WE'RE AFRAID.

Before we ask the question, "Are we up against people or Satan?" the book of Exodus demands we ask a more visceral question, one that many of our pieties have trouble admitting we struggle with: "Are we up against people or *God*?" When the circumstances are deteriorating instead of improving, especially if we're doing all we can to faithfully align ourselves with Jesus' prayer and priorities, some vexing doubts can surface. Check out who Exodus describes as the cause of all the Israelites' trouble:

- "And I will harden Pharaoh's heart, and he will pursue them." (Exodus 14:4)

- "The Lord hardened the heart of Pharaoh king of Egypt, so that he pursued the Israelites, who were marching out boldly." (Exodus 14:8)

- "I will harden the hearts of the Egyptians so that they will go in after them. And I will gain glory through Pharaoh and all his army, through his chariots and his horsemen." (Exodus 14:17)

Pharaoh's arteriosclerosis is mentioned 17 times in the book of Exodus. Here's what's fascinating: ten times, *God* did it; four times it says, "His heart became hard;" three times we read that

Pharaoh hardened his own heart. All seven initiated by Pharaoh are in the middle of the story. In the beginning and the end, God's in charge, but in the heat of the battle, we have a part to play in the choices we make. Aren't you glad that God's in charge so that while we have free will, it has limits? I'd find it completely terrifying if God gave us free will with absolutely no limitations. We're *never* up against God, even when it may seem like it. Romans 8:31–32 assures, "If God is for us, who can be against us? ³²He who did not spare his own Son, but gave him up for us all—how will he not also, along with him, graciously give us all things?" God is emphatically for us.

So there is a foe—but it isn't God, and the enemy's powers are limited. Knowing that, we can then return to the original question: "Are we up against people or Satan?" People will often quip, "The devil made me do it," ignoring personal responsibility for the decisions we make. The devil didn't make Pharaoh harden his heart, though he undoubtedly was cheering him on. Ephesians 6 explicitly tells us that our battle ultimately is not against flesh and blood, meaning other people. We'll much more likely resolve the brushfires of conflict that Satan is trying to fan into full flame if we remember that Satan is the enemy, not the person across the table who loves the same Lord we do, even if the current circumstances feel less like "iron sharpening iron" and more like a street fight with tire irons. Satan constantly strives to divide and conquer. We're called to constantly resist his efforts.

3. *Fear and faith: who are you talking to?* In Exodus 14:11–12, the Israelites said to Moses, "Was it because there were no graves in Egypt that you brought us out to the desert to die? What have you done to us by bringing us out of Egypt? ¹²Didn't we say to you in Egypt, 'Leave us alone; let us serve the Egyptians'? It would have been better for us to serve the Egyptians than to die in the desert!" The phrase "irrational fear" is a misnomer. Fear itself isn't irrational; sometimes it's irrational to not be afraid.

Teenagers wouldn't do many of the things they do if they had a little more rational fear; drivers wouldn't drive impaired if they realized what their thousands-of-pounds hunk of metal could do to a person crossing the street in front of them. But fear can make us say irrational things we'd otherwise never speak if we weren't scared out of our minds. After the Red Sea crossing, multiple encores of fear-infested finger pointing played out. Our enemy is Satan, and while he can't defeat us, he'll certainly be happy to neutralize us with fear—if we allow him.

The key question is, "Who do you talk to when you're afraid?" The people first took their fear to each other. Then, when their grumble stew reached a boil, they went after Moses. Was Moses as afraid as the people were? Yes—and not only did he have the Egyptians, dehydration, and hunger to fear, he had to be afraid of the people, too. But Moses took his fears to God every single time. The difference between walking in fear and walking in faith is sometimes as simple as who we talk to when we're afraid.

Fear is a crossroad experience. Fear in a group can either drive them together or tear them apart. If the whole group recognizes that the danger is big but God is bigger, and then if that same group turns to God in prayer, their fear can unite them. But it's far more common to see fear accomplish the opposite—and as soon as people start grumbling against one another or against their leaders, the original danger pales in comparison to the new one. Jesus says, "Blessed are those who mourn." It's appropriate to share our fears with others as long as our listeners help us take those fears to God rather than reflect and amplify them. Mourning is different than venting; be careful of venting to others and giving voice to the enemy. As the song says of God, "You are my hiding place. You always fill my heart with songs of deliverance. Whenever I am afraid I will trust in You. I will trust in You. Let the weak say I am strong in the strength of the Lord."

4.   Freeze, then follow. Moses answered the Israelites in Exodus 14:13–14. "Do not be afraid. Stand firm and you will see the deliverance the Lord will bring you today. The Egyptians you see today you will never see again. [14]The Lord will fight for you; you need only to be still."

Be still. Freeze. Our part, next to God's part, is nothing. God-sized problems require God-sized solutions. Have you ever wondered why it seems like more miracles today take place elsewhere than in America? One significant reason is that there are fewer options in other parts of the world. It's harder to see God heal the blind when laser surgery will do it. Is God still the healer? Absolutely—He's limited neither by the presence of the medical field nor the lack of it. Our ability to show *how* God worked, through human agents or scientifically-explained activity, changes nothing about the ultimate cause.

WHEN HE SAYS, "HERE'S HOW YOU CAN HELP," LET'S SAY YES— EVEN IF IT SEEMS SMALL AND INSIGNIFICANT OR HUGE AND SCARY.

Yet again God usually gives us a part to play, much like parents who let their young children "help." When Jesus advocates for faith like a child, He wants us to emulate a child's unabashed desire to help and be part of the action. In the case of the Red Sea, no committee could have figured out a way through—but God still told Moses to reach out his staff over the edge of the sea; He still told the Israelites to put one foot in front of the other and walk into a sea bed with water piled high a few feet away on either side. God never promised to pick them up and transport them to the other side. He just made the way. They still had to move.

After the Israelites crossed the sea, do you suppose Moses said, "Look what I did! I lifted up my staff, and just like that, whammo, the waters divided. I was amazing!" I doubt it. Moses' part next to God's part was nothing—and yet the wonder of wonders is that God waited for Moses to do his insignificant part as an act of obedience before He did the heavy lifting.

God doesn't need our help; our first problem is we often forget that. But God invites us to participate; our second problem is we often forget that, too. Let's not get a big head and think God won't get very far if not for our help. Freeze—for even with things we can solve, we must check in with the Boss and see if that's even where He wants us working. Follow—so that when He parts the sea in front of us, we walk through it. When He says, "Here's how you can help," let's say yes—even if it seems small and insignificant or huge and scary.

PRAYER: WHERE GOD'S PART AND OUR PART MEET

Prayer includes not only what we say to God, but what He says to us. When we hear Him say, "Lift the staff," we do it without needing to understand it. When we hear Him say, "Walk through the sea," we place our fears in His hands and walk. Desperation also provides tremendous fodder for prayer, and divine discontent fuels prayer like little else. More than once, the Exodus story tells us how beaten down the Israelites became, normalizing their slavery to where they lost hope it could ever change. Even *after* they were free, they sometimes whitewashed their history and looked back at their years in slavery with longing simply because it was familiar. God must often point out how far we've fallen and how unacceptable our present circumstances are for us to reach a desperation point where we cry out to Him, "How long, O Lord?" Then we're willing to obey, even if His next step seems as miniscule as, "Hold out your staff."

The incredible transformational stories of churches partnering with public education and the foster care system from Chapter 6 were born out of desperation. If forming a committee could have solved it or if human solutions held out any hope of changing things, turning to God might have seemed less appealing. The truth is there are so many situations right now in our communities that need God-sized solutions, the opportunities for unity/harmony to flourish are abundant! But God's part and our part must meet first. That happens through prayer.

Mark Harris says that in the early days of 4Tucson, when our domain wheel was first rolled out, one of the most common questions was the reason for a Prayer Domain. Some asked, "Doesn't prayer belong in everything? Why have a separate domain just for prayer?" The answer, of course, is that prayer does belong in everything—and that's why it is its own domain. We must never forget that apart from God we can do nothing. 4Tucson Prayer Domain Director Brian Goodall watches what the other domains are doing and regularly intervenes with, "How can we partner in prayer with you?" If you go back and re-read the two stories of church-school partnerships and DCS-church partnerships, you'll see the indispensable role that prayer played in both.

Brian now teaches an eight-week transformational prayer course at churches around the city. His second lesson asks the question regarding prayer, "What is God's responsibility and what is our responsibility?" and the rest of this section draws heavily from that content. In that class, he confronts the common misconception that it's *our* job to do all the work. People often quote 2 Rumors 3:17, "God helps those who help themselves," a saying that isn't in the Bible. These people typically believe prayer doesn't accomplish anything. Another misconception is that it's God's job to do all the work. Just pray, some say, and God will take care of everything. These people pray for provision, but refuse to ask for help from others, tighten their budget, or learn to be better stewards of their resources. They'll pray for a friend's salvation, but never share the love of Jesus. I've often wondered how many of our prayers God marks, "Return to sender," saying, "That's your job."

Jesus tells the disciples in John 4:35 to notice that the fields are "ripe for harvest" spiritually. He had just shocked them in His encounter with the Samaritan woman at the well, who had three societal strikes against her—she was a woman, a Samaritan, and a five-time divorcee now living with a sixth partner. The disciples were satisfied with the status quo, the current state of brokenness that left many on the outside looking in.

But Jesus wasn't, initiating the conversation that led to an entire village coming to know Him. In a different context, Jesus uses a similar analogy. In Matthew 9:37, Jesus tells His disciples, "The harvest is plentiful but the workers are few." The next verse illustrates well the God's part/our part dynamic. He neither instructs them to move straight to a solution without consulting God first in prayer, nor does He tell them to pray but never become part of the solution. It's out of that season of prayer that the disciple learn *where* to go. If we forget to pray, we're likely going to head out on our own assignment and in our own strength. In addition, if we don't listen in prayer, we won't hear His answer, and we'll likely stay on our knees when God is trying to lift us to our feet. God gives us the assignment, tells us where and how to go, and then fills us with His Spirit as we go.

> **I'VE OFTEN WONDERED HOW MANY OF OUR PRAYERS GOD MARKS, "RETURN TO SENDER," SAYING, "THAT'S YOUR JOB."**

Next, Brian discusses prayer as a partnership. There are things we can control and things that are out of our control. In the amazing post-Easter story of John 21:1–11, the disciples aren't sure what to do next, so they go fishing. They labor all night but catch nothing. Jesus then shows up on the shore, but they don't recognize Him. He tells them to throw their net on the other side of the boat—and the miraculous catch nearly swamps the boat. What changed from the moment the disciples set out to fish to the moment they hauled in the huge net? Everything was the same as every other time before—same people, same lake, same location, same method, same net, same time, same fish, same boat, same weather—except that Jesus spoke. When they heard Jesus' instruction, everything changed. The lesson for the disciples that morning was the same He had shared with them just a couple of weeks earlier. "Remain in me, as I also remain in you. No branch can bear fruit by itself; it must remain in the vine. Neither can you bear fruit unless you remain in me. ⁵"I am the vine; you are the branches. If you remain in me and I in you, you will bear much fruit; apart from me you can do nothing." (John 15:4–5) Our responsibility is to remain in Jesus! We will only be as effective as our willingness to abide in Him and rely on His voice above our skills, experiences, and resources.

Flash forward several weeks, and we observe another miracle. The disciples learned the lesson! Which means that we can, too! Acts 4:13 records this remarkable observation made by religious leaders and others: "When they saw the courage of Peter and John and realized they were unschooled, ordinary men, they were astonished and they took note these men had been with Jesus."

Brian concludes the lesson by showing the group how to pray Scripture, calling the practice the most practical application to what Jesus said when He told His disciples to remain in Him. The more we pray Scripture, the better we will be at discerning Jesus' voice. When we pray Scripture, we are responding directly to God's own words; we are grafting ourselves into the values that are important to God, expressions of His character, promises that communicate His heart, truth that demonstrates His nature, and principles that align us with His will. Dietrich Bonhoeffer writes, "If we wish to pray with confidence and gladness, then the words of the Holy Scriptures will have to be the solid basis of our prayer. For here we know that Jesus Christ, the Word of God, teaches us to pray. The words that come from God become, then, the steps on which we find our way to God."[3]

Our responsibility is to pray—and this means more than simply spending some time with God each morning. Certainly, it's good to devote time to being in God's presence with no distractions. Yet prayer isn't to be a spiritual compartment in our life; it's to be our way of life, where our whole day is spent constantly and consistently communing with God, asking Him to help us see what He sees and respond as He responds. God is responsible for the results, and the Holy Spirit will help us when we feel overwhelmed or incapacitated. "The Holy Spirit helps us in our weakness." (Romans 8:26) The Greek word for "weakness" is *astheneia*, which means "without strength or ability," so that we

---

3   *Psalms: The Prayer Book of the Bible*, by Dietrich Bonhoeffer.

can translate, "The Spirit helps us with our inability to produce results." What a powerful partnership prayer produces!

THE LORD'S TWO PRAYERS

The Lord's Prayer is what most of Christianity calls Matthew 6:9–13, where Jesus taught about prayer. The Lord's Prayer, in other words, is the most prominent pattern for prayer that Jesus *taught*. John 17 is the most prominent prayer that Jesus *prayed*.

The two are not synonymous, but neither are they incompatible. Notice how the prayer that Jesus taught is congruent with the prayer that Jesus prayed:

> WE WILL ONLY BE AS EFFECTIVE AS OUR WILLINGNESS TO ABIDE IN HIM AND RELY ON HIS VOICE ABOVE OUR SKILLS, EXPERIENCES, AND RESOURCES.

- *Our Father.* Most noteworthy is that Jesus taught His disciples to pray from a corporate perspective rather than an individual perspective, even if they were praying by themselves. We don't address prayer to *my* Father, but *our* Father. The first word points to the unity/harmony that Jesus later prayed.

- *Thy kingdom come.* The Kingdom of God is compared to yeast that works its way through the entire batch of dough. The Kingdom of God is always bigger than one congregation, one network/denomination, one ethnicity, or any other singular perspective.

- *As it is in Heaven.* In Heaven, every nation, tribe, language, and people will be gathered together before the throne of God (Revelation 5:9 and 14:6). If we're going to pray as Jesus taught, that His kingdom would come and His will be done on Earth as it is in Heaven, unity/harmony here on Earth is the rehearsal for the perfect unity/harmony that we'll later experience in Heaven.

- *As we forgive those who trespass against us.* Sin divides; forgiveness reconciles. Jesus taught us to pray not only for our own forgiveness, but that we would be forgiven in the same manner we forgive others. Division is not acceptable because the Cross breaks down all the barriers.

- *Thine is the glory.* Many parts of Christianity add a later doxology to the pattern Jesus taught in Matthew 6: "for thine is the kingdom, and the power, and the glory, forever and ever, Amen." That doxology begins by recognizing that the glory belongs to God, not to us.

Prayer is the place where God's part and our part meet, especially when prayer is not merely a spiritual compartment, but the cry of a heart out of the circumstances of life. Praying back to God His own Word is a very effective way to be transformed by the renewing of our minds (Romans 12:2). When we pray as Jesus taught, a significant part of that pattern reflects what Jesus later prayed at His point of greatest need.

OUR PART INCLUDES SEEKING AND SERVING GOD

My wife and I have been using the popular devotional *Jesus Calling* in addition to our own Bible reading plans. The February 7 entry caught my attention in the context of God's part/our part:

> Seek My Face more and more. You are really just beginning your journey of intimacy with Me. It is not an easy road, but it is a delightful and privileged way: a treasure hunt. I am the Treasure, and the Glory of My Presence glistens and shimmers along the way. Hardships are part of the journey too. I mete them out ever so carefully, in just the right dosage, with a tenderness you can hardly imagine. Do not recoil from afflictions, since they are among My most favored gifts. *Trust Me and don't be afraid, for I am your Strength and Song (Isaiah 12:2).*[4]

---

4   *Jesus Calling,* by Sarah Young.

We are to make seeking the Lord a priority. In the story of Mary and Martha in Luke 10:38–42, Martha is slaving away in the kitchen while Mary is hanging on Jesus' every word in the living room. In His exhortation to Martha that Mary has chosen "what is better," Jesus doesn't conclude that we're never to serve; rather, He shows that unless we're taking our cues from Him, we'll burn out in our own strength and likely lose unity/harmony with those we love in the process. God alone can show us when, where, and how to serve effectively while giving us the fuel to live on.

When Ephesians 2:8–9 says, "For it is by grace you have been saved, through faith—and this is not from yourselves, it is the gift of God—⁹not by works, so that no one can boast," it is not saying our responsibility in the Christian life is to sit back and relax, doing nothing. After all, verse 10 follows, "For we are God's handiwork, created in Christ Jesus to do good works, which God prepared in advance for us to do." We are to seek and then serve. Likewise, when Philippians 2:12 says, "Therefore, my dear friends, as you have always obeyed—not only in my presence, but now much more in my absence—continue to work out your salvation with fear and trembling," it is not saying that salvation is our job. That's why verse 13 follows with, "for it is God who works in you to will and to act in order to fulfill his good purpose." He longs for our service after we have sought Him for strength and wisdom.

Prayer isn't a formula, it's a relationship. While we learn and grow in praying more effectively, the point isn't to learn a bunch of rules so that we can pray the right way. Praying together as pastors at Pastor Prayer Summits has been enormously unifying, as has talking together as pastors in our Pastors Partnership meetings. Through both praying and talking together, we're learning how to rely on God and seek and serve Him better than we could on our own.

Our Pastors Partnership meetings together during the 2016 presidential election had some sparks. We concluded in the first meeting after the election that we wanted to devote more time together to prayer and fasting. We had planned to watch a movie together that month, but

God had a better plan and prevented the movie from working! Talking and praying together was much more engaging than watching a movie would have been. We all agreed that in our city and country, we're desperate for God to move in ways that only He can. As we've continued to operationalize these intentions, I jotted down several comments and prayers from our December 2016 gathering. Listen to how the transparent atmosphere of unity/harmony led us to keep growing deeper and deeper. Pastor Tony Moss confessed, "God, you called us a 'house of prayer,' but there's not much prayer." Pastor Demetrius Miles shared how his congregation was founded on prayer, but in recent years has experienced mission drift. Another pastor commented, "You can't engineer a movement, you have to pray it down from Heaven." Someone pointed out that the famous 2 Chronicles 7:14 verse isn't directed to the nation, it's directed to us: if "my" people. Apostle Jamie Benjamin shared about the biblical figures of Ezra, Nehemiah, and Jerubbabel, concluding that God alone can grant us favor, but we must faithfully carry out our assignments. Pastor Dan Johnson prayed regarding our need for discernment, noting that even healthy branches are pruned away and desiring to recognize the good-without-God in our lives that needs pruning. Pastor Jim Cords talked about how we're called to share our lives with faith being evident rather than just share our faith and keep our lives at bay. By the end of the meeting, we made plans to observe President Trump's inauguration day by meeting, eating, praying, and worshiping together.

WHAT A POWERFUL PARTNERSHIP PRAYER PRODUCES!

Allowing Jesus' own prayer in John 17 to become leaven for the entire loaf of our lives will help us align with Jesus' surprising strategy for revealing His love for our world. In the next chapter, we'll look at the unfortunate tendency to foolishly choose sides where the "sides" are really part of the same team.

QUESTIONS FOR SELF-REFLECTION

- What insights do you want to hold onto from Exodus 13–14? How will you "operationalize" them?

- Have you ever seen fear play a role in the (potential) fracturing of unity/harmony? What happened?

- How have you seen desperation help your prayer life? Does desperation always lead to greater trust and dependence on God? If not, what's the difference between when it does and when it doesn't?

- Where are the growing edges of your prayer life? How is prayer helping you more effectively partner with God?

TODAY'S GPS

Lord Jesus, we desire to glorify You in every stage of our lives. When we're in exciting seasons of harvest, may we give all the praise and honor to You, never attempting to keep some of the spoils for ourselves. And when we're in seasons of great trial and testing, help us honor You by taking our fears to You. Protect us from the enemy who misleads us to freeze when You've told us to follow, or follow when You've told us to freeze. Protect us from the enemy who seeks to separate our work from Yours, or Your work from ours. Teach us what it means to partner with You as we pray back to You the Word You've given to us. Sanctify us in Your truth, and help us to consistently seek and serve You. Help us grow in our reliance and trust in You, for You are good beyond measure. Amen.

Chapter Eight

OUR BIG FAT GREEK PROBLEM: HOW WESTERN THINKING THREATENS UNITY

IF it was easy to reverse two millennia of thought and philosophy, I might just set out to do that. Thank God that there is a God, and He's not me.

We're too Greek. Nothing against Greeks, as my son-in-law is one, but the kind of Greek I'm talking about is our Western way of thinking that is foreign to the biblical homeland.

BOTH/AND, NOT EITHER/OR

Hebrew thinking is both/and thinking. Psalm 89:14 is indicative: "Righteousness and justice are the foundation of your throne; love and faithfulness go before you." For many of us, when we picture a "God of love" and then visualize a "God of justice," the two images don't evoke the same portrait. The Bible consistently affirms that God is omnipotent (all powerful, with nothing outside His realm) as well as all-loving (always good, with love as His identity, not just one part of His character). When we read texts like we did in the last chapter from the book of Exodus that say that God hardened Pharaoh's heart, we immediately react, "How fair is that?" That's because we're too Greek in our thinking.

Greek thinking is either/or thinking. Either God is all-powerful or God is all-loving, but since those appear to contradict each other, He can't be both. Greek thinking has infiltrated our culture to the extent that a mere statement can be assumed to be on an either/or trajectory that leads to ideas that the speaker never intended. For example, pick someone out in a room and give them a compliment, and it's likely that someone else in the room will think, "Why don't they like or appreciate me?" As if compliments are a zero-sum game where each one must be balanced out by a criticism. That's either/or thinking at work.[1]

The Old Testament was written in Hebrew and the New Testament was written in Greek. But that's deceiving when it comes to the topic at hand because all the authors of the New Testament were Jewish. Both Testaments come from a Jewish mindset, not a Greek one. When John 1:14 says that Jesus came "full of grace and truth," that's a Hebrew mindset at work, a both/and rather than an either/or.

At first glance, it might appear that post-modernity is making a move back toward Hebrew thinking. Many today don't seem to be too bothered if someone points out that beliefs or values they're espousing are mutually contradictory. For example, many of the strongest proponents of inclusivity will quickly exclude those whose beliefs don't match theirs. They're operating out of two convictions that conflict: that all points of view are equally valid and should be validated, and that a belief in an absolute that delineates between right and wrong is a threat to an inclusive culture. Is this both/and thinking at work?

I don't think so. To illustrate, Hebrew thinking loves dichotomies—contrasts between two items that at first glance appear to be mutually

---

1   This difference between Hebrew and Greek worldview has been addressed in a variety of ways, such as Linear (Greek) versus Box (Hebrew) Logic, by Tim Hegg (http://messianic-publications.com/tim-hegg/my-big-fat-greek-mindset-part-1), and Circular versus Linear by N'tan Lawrence, "Hebrew thought compared with Greek (Western) Thought: a Key to Understanding Scripture through the Eyes of the Authors."

exclusive. These dichotomies hold in tension grace and truth, as well as love and justice, so that by refusing to allow one to cancel out the other, both are brought to their fullest expression. Rather than choosing one over the other, Hebrew thinking sees both attributes working in harmony toward a greater goal. That strikes me as very different than logical fallacies that lead us to a place of nonsense and often an excuse for irresponsibility. One of the most helpful pieces of training I received in biblical study, preaching, and life came from my home pastor, Mark Reitan, who taught me to see the point of tension in a biblical text, sit there prayerfully on the horns of the dilemma, and watch for new insights to emerge that align with other scriptural truth.

Romans 13:10 is a tremendous case study in the difference between Greek and Hebrew thinking, packed with very contemporary societal implications. "Love does no harm to a neighbor. Therefore love is the fulfillment of the law." Greek

> WHEN THE BODY OF CHRIST DIVIDES UP AND TAKES SIDES, THE SPLIT CAN USUALLY BE TRACED TO THIS EITHER/OR THINKING INSTEAD OF BOTH/AND.

thinking immediately sets out to pit "love" and "the law" against one another. Thus, "fulfillment of the law" and "overturning of the law" become synonymous. The thinking goes that as long as people are acting out of love, how they express that love can't be ruled as wrong. This leads to some outrageous conclusions. If an adult man believes he loves a five-year-old girl, should he be free to act on that love sexually, since love and the law are either/or, with love trumping the law?[2] The Greek word for "fulfill" (πληρόω *pleroo*), however, isn't synonymous with "overturn" or "negate," but rather means "to bring to fullest expression." This verse isn't saying that love is the new "law" rendering all previous law outdated and of no value. Paul is arguing the opposite: love will always bring the law to its fullest expression. If we start using the law to justify ourselves, as in "we

---

2   This is not an imagined example, but the story of Todd Nickerson, as discussed in the video https://www.youtube.com/watch?v=vJZWNkJrKJc

did this and that, and refrained from this and that, therefore we must have been showing love," love goes deeper than the law can ever fully articulate; love brings specific commandments to their fullest understanding and expression. This line of both/and thinking is thoroughly consistent with Jesus' own words from Matthew 5:17, where He says, "Do not think that I have come to abolish the Law or the Prophets: I have not come to abolish them but to fulfill them." Jesus then illustrates throughout the rest of Matthew 5 how love and the law are both/and, not either/or.

Antinomianism (literally "against the law") was deemed a heresy by the early Christian church, even though that heresy can be seen resurrecting itself in post-modern thinking that, sadly, has infiltrated parts of the Church. Either/or thinking contributes to our immaturity, as discussed in Chapter 2. The reason antinomianism is sometimes not seen as anti-biblical traces not only to our Greek thinking, but our lack of unity. Continuing with the Romans 13:10 example, we see people clinging to the "law" and proving to be judgmental and usually hypocritical in the process. That's rightfully repulsive, so we swing the pendulum to the other ditch and assume that it's incompatible to love someone and simultaneously tell them they're wrong, even though every parent worth the title knows how essential it is to do exactly that. I'm convinced that a mature balance of grace and truth, love and the law, unity/harmony and doctrinal integrity, could prove so attractive to so many that a Christian Church that truly practiced it would once again function as preservative salt for the culture, flavoring it instead of following it.

When the body of Christ divides up and takes sides, the split can usually be traced to this either/or thinking instead of both/and. Many of the following points made in previous chapters reveal a common trend when combined and looked at from a Hebrew perspective.

- When Jesus gave new meaning to the Passover meal at the Last Supper by transforming a Jewish rite into Christian Holy Communion, did He intend to be taken seriously when He said, "This is my body . . . this is my blood" or "Do this in remembrance of me?" It doesn't have to be either/or. Wars were fought and people killed over the mistaken belief that truth could only be obtained in one or the other perspective.

• Is racism an individual or systemic issue? Remember, both the individual pieces and the big picture are required to assemble a puzzle. Individual racist tendencies, overt or otherwise, must be examined, but so must inequitable systems that favor one group over another for no valid reason.

• Should we worship God with awe and reverence or with emotion and participation? This is just one example of many of the "worship wars" congregations have struggled with for decades. Cultural differences and preferences are real and part of God's design, and a both/and citywide perspective can make it possible for everyone to worship God in their heart languages without a competitive atmosphere that confuses personal preference with divine preference.

• Is (fill in the blank) in the sacred or secular realm? Sacred/secular dualism is perhaps the clearest example of Greek thinking that runs counter to a biblical worldview. God regularly invades the commonplace ("secular") with His presence ("sacred"). Simultaneously, sin continues to infect all Christ-followers so that our actions and motives are never 100 percent pure. The classic Reformation framing of this both/and perspective is that Christians are simultaneously saint and sinner.

• Does God heal supernaturally or naturally? Whenever the two are split apart in either/or fashion, those doing the splitting miss out on the vastness of God's healing activity. Taken to an extreme, limiting God to the supernatural can cause people to die when God has provided a means for healing, and limiting God to the natural can cause people to turn medicine and science into a god that can't possibly deliver on the hope and values ascribed to them.

- Should we make decisions by reason or revelation? To live by reason or common sense alone ends up becoming complete self-reliance. Many of the paths God calls us to walk don't make much sense to limited human foresight. Sometimes we come to a place where we can look back and see more of what God saw, and other times that level of understanding may not happen until Heaven. But to live only by revelation—believing that unless God tells us something directly, we shouldn't decide—is to deny the stewardship and maturity for which God makes us responsible. "Should I get out of bed today, Lord? I'll wait for your answer" is likely unrealistic, but praying about a potential employee instead of checking references is an all-too-common example.

> YET ANOTHER GREEK INVASION CONCERNS THE MYTH THAT RENEWAL AND TRANSFORMATION SHOULD BE EITHER ORGANIC OR STRUCTURED, AS IF THE TWO WERE MUTUALLY EXCLUSIVE.

- Are problems we encounter due to spiritual warfare or human sin? To blame everything on the devil and his minions is to fail to take responsibility for our own actions and inactions. To ignore the spiritual realm and forget that we have an enemy is to fail to armor up in the middle of a battleground. Both failures can be avoided by not falling into the either/or trap.

- When thinking about relational unity/harmony and working through conflict, should we apply that at a citywide level or a congregational one? To be sure, there can be a tension between taking relational commitment seriously at a congregational level versus a citywide one. If unity is only applied congregationally, we fail to recognize God's hand in moving people strategically to different parts of the same body in the citywide Church. If unity is only applied citywide, we fail to recognize God's hand in helping people grow and mature by working through the conflicts right where they are.

- In the Sacraments of Baptism and Holy Communion, is God making promises or are we? Viewpoints on baptism and communion often reflect twin pillars when it comes to salvation: 1) we are saved by grace through faith, apart from works of the law; it's God's doing, and 2) humans respond to God's grace by accepting and applying it or rejecting and ignoring it. Some viewpoints on baptism and communion emphasize God's part, while others emphasize ours. I don't have a problem with landing at some point on the spectrum (a congregation choosing to baptize babies—all God's part—or not) so long as we don't end up in the Greek thinking that says we have to break fellowship with those having an opposing view.

- Should congregations biblically accept women operating in the same levels of leadership as men? That does become an either/or question at some point, but making a decision doesn't necessitate ending relationship with those who reach a *different* decision based on their interpretation of the Bible. At our Pastor Prayer Summits, we've encouraged everyone to allow each congregation to define "pastor" according to their own scriptural view, and have reached a place of mutual respect and acceptance of one another.

- Congregations that do well at discerning their particular mission and outreach niches need to remember that corporate mission and personal mission aren't either/or, but both/and. Not every passion of every individual is one that God calls the entire congregation to adopt, but a both/and perspective creates an environment where individuals are encouraged to pursue their callings by linking arms with other parts of the citywide Body of Christ. Clear congregational focus and an empowering atmosphere belong together, not in opposition.

Does Jesus pray for our protection from the enemy because Satan's chief strategy is to divide and conquer, or does Satan constantly seek to divide and conquer because Jesus prayed for unity/harmony? Probably both. The topic of unity/harmony is challenged by Greek thinking right from the outset because unity/harmony and truth are so often pitted against one another instead of held together in a more Hebrew mindset. Whether the pursuit is doctrinal truth, moral truth, or simply the most important priorities, perspectives, or methodologies, the pursuit of the best does not have to clash with unity/harmony. I'm more convinced than ever that if unity/harmony and truth are separated from one another, both are lost.

THE MISSING MIDDLE: WHO ELSE IS DOING THIS?

At one time Tucson had the highest number of nonprofits per capita of any city in the nation, according to Randy Reynolds of Community Renewal—and I believe that's both a blessing and a curse. On the upside, it shows we have many trailblazers in the Old Pueblo, pioneers unafraid to start something new. Most nonprofits are started in response to a need, often one that has personally touched the founder/visionary. Parents of special needs children benefit from a support group; single moms need a way to earn a college degree; sex trafficking must be identified and prevented, and its victims given the opportunity to be rescued and rehabilitated; the refugee crisis around the globe has a personal face to it down the street. All these and hundreds more are examples of people allowing God to use one of their areas of greatest heartbreak and turn it into a ministry. Tucson is filled with compassionate people who want to make a positive difference and contribution—so much so that in 2014 Tucson was identified as the third most caring city in the nation.[3]

The not-so-good side of that statistic is what I call the missing middle. Here's how it usually goes:

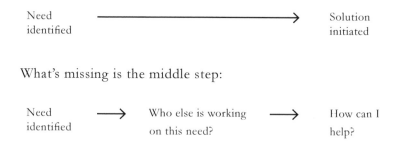

---

3   http://www.movoto.com/blog/top-ten/most-caring-cities-in-america/

Many nonprofits are small, often one person operations struggling to keep the doors open. Many people notice the same need but then create their own solution, and the duplication of service and effort hinders progress. Different parts of the Body of Christ quickly find themselves competing with one another for the resources and compassion of the community. If only we could figure out that we're better *together*, we could use the passion, experience, and energy God has given to *us* to support the same passion, experience, and energy He gave someone *else*. We might not approach meeting the need the same way, but that can almost always be an asset instead of a liability. If we're willing to work through some of the conflict, we can special-

FIRST CENTURY CHURCH FOUND TO BE RACIST: GREEKS FILE LAWSUIT OVER FOOD DISCRIMINATION.

ize and arrive at whole new levels of unity/harmony and maturity. For a time, when meeting with various churches and nonprofits around town, I found myself regularly encountering the missing middle syndrome. At some point when I couldn't take it anymore, I'd say, "Just one request: 'Please don't start something new!'" One of the great gifts of being able to give full-time attention to what God's doing in our city is discovering His activity through people all over town, and helping others connect the dots when they express similar passions.

How Greek is this missing middle? We've bought into the lie that we must choose between creativity and order, ingenuity and collaboration, leadership and subordination. Being one's own boss has appeal, but in a Christian worldview, we're never really our own bosses anyway. What if God is calling us to work together instead of independently? What if He left Heaven to deliver that message personally in the form of a John 17 prayer? It will take more maturity, but it *is* possible for strong, independently-minded leaders to work together on the same project instead of going off in different directions. Plus, when this happens, we'll find ourselves glorifying the Son, resisting the devil, maturing the flesh, and working *with* God instead of against Him. Jesus' prayer can truly be our GPS.

My wife and I have four young adult children; five if you count our son-in-law, which we happily do. Parenting takes on new challenges and blessings at every stage, and the missing middle causes many problems. If one of us sees a problem and initiates a solution without consulting the other—without asking "who else is working on this need"—a high probability exists that one of us is going to have to backtrack and clean up new messes that could have been avoided. Valerie and I bring very different gifts and temperaments to our parenting, but we've found that if we each use our specialties while collaborating on the front end, instead of trying to function in an identical manner, the issues are addressed much more successfully. I'm sure we'll have it down perfectly by our golden anniversary.

ORGANIC OR STRUCTURED?

Yet another Greek invasion concerns the myth that renewal and transformation should be either organic or structured, as if the two were mutually exclusive. In my homiletics (the art of preaching or writing sermons) class in seminary, some students emphasized the importance of being led by the Spirit, while others focused on the importance of preparation. Yet we don't have to choose between the two. Those who were exclusively led by the Spirit often repackaged the same content; it was fiery, but familiar. Those who were exquisitely prepared were often about as exciting as watching paint dry; it might have been great stuff, but you had to stay awake to get to it. Spontaneous isn't synonymous with spiritual, nor does preparation guarantee delivery.

The events of Acts 2 were quite organic. Jesus had told His twelve to wait for the outpouring of the Holy Spirit, knowing that if they relied on their own strength, the Church would never get off the ground, let alone fly. Nobody of human origin planned what happened on that Day of Pentecost as 3,000 new believers in Jesus as Messiah were gained from a sermon Peter hadn't planned to preach. Some structure for the newborn Church started to show up in those early weeks (Acts 2:42–47), even while the organic river kept flowing, as recorded in subsequent chapters. By Acts 6, some further organization was essential or the movement could have flamed out prematurely. God was moving on so many fronts that the apostles were falling victim to the tyranny of the urgent. Burnout was brewing. Roles needed to be defined and new leaders identified. Important ministries were being neglected, and complaints were growing. "In those days when the number of disciples was increasing, the Hellenistic Jews among them complained against the Hebraic Jews because their widows were being overlooked in the daily distribution of food." (Acts 6:1) The headline *First century church found to be racist: Greeks file lawsuit over food discrimination* could have proven deadly. Did you notice the requirement for the food distributors? They had to be "full of the Spirit and wisdom." (Acts 6:3) Structure was not seen as being anti-spiritual, nor was administration seen as no longer relying on the Holy Spirit. The result of the intervention and implementation of some structure? "The word of God spread. The number of disciples in Jerusalem increased rapidly, and a large number of priests became obedient to the faith." (Acts 6:7) Multiplication became possible by marrying an organic movement with structure and combining the Spirit with wisdom.

WITHOUT LEADERSHIP, NO MOVEMENT WILL LAST FOR LONG.

Yet too much structure, too many policies, and too much rigidity is just as deadly. When God opens up the Red Sea right in front of us, it shouldn't take an act of Congress to get us to move through it. Nobody starts out with the goal of creating a bureaucracy. When I was involved in the formation of Lutheran Congregations in Mission for Christ, a new national network of congregations starting in 2001, we constantly coached each other to "avoid institutional creep"—meaning to always be on the lookout for self-serving and/or unnecessary policies and procedures. But when unhealthy pastors starting looking to our organization as an attractive place to land, given how lean and green we were, the necessity of some structure became obvious. We needed some policies and procedures to help congregations protect themselves from wolves dressed in sheep's clothing.

The human body provides a great analogy for the relationship between organic and structured. Bodies are an amazing combination of cells that form limbs, organs, and systems. Supporting it all and holding it all together is a skeleton. When you look at a body, it's not the skeleton you want to see; if bones are showing, that's a problem in and of itself. But the body isn't going anywhere without a skeleton supporting it.

One danger of too much centralized structure can be that only those at the top discern God's will and carry out His ministry, while everyone else merely serves in support positions. Yet everyone in the Body of Christ is a stakeholder; 1 Corinthians 12 is clear that there are no irrelevant body parts in the Church of Jesus Christ. Pastor Jim Toole of St. Andrews Presbyterian Church in Tucson wrote in his doctoral dissertation, "Decentralization, in this paper, is defined as a church empowering change through laity rather than staff . . . Decentralization comes about by creating a church culture of permission and even at times a bit of chaos to allow missional experimentation to seep out to the greater congregation. St. Andrews Presbyterian in Tucson is allowing its members to create, experiment, and propose entrepreneurial missional opportunities. It is a bit more chaotic, stressful, and unpredictable; however, the congregational culture is truly changing, not from the staff but from the very people themselves." An organic perspective guards against leaning too heavily on the "our part" side of the God's part/our part dialectic.

A notable concern for those operating in an organic environment is the pride that manifests itself in a lack of willingness to submit to anyone else's leadership. Authoritarian, prideful leadership needs to be resisted, and Jesus both demonstrated and directly taught a different style of servant leadership (See Mark 10:42–45). Without leadership, no movement will last for long. As I've met leaders from different city transformation movements around the country, one of the most commonly cited factors in the growth and maturity of a city movement is its leadership. Personality driven congregations and citywide organizations that lack structure tend to only last as long as that leader does. Leadership and structure that empower everyone to carry out their roles is the very definition of maturity from Ephesians 4, as cited in Chapter 2. Structure and organization are not the enemy of the Spirit if all recognize that the Head of the Church is allowed to call the shots and overturn our tables whenever He deems it necessary.

COMMUNICATION CONUNDRUMS

When it comes to our physical body, how does the head communicate with the rest of the body? How do the body parts coordinate with one another? Neuroscientists today can explain how neurons are cells specialized for communication, and synapses are junctions through which neurons can communicate with other neurons and other types of cells through electrical impulses. The human brain alone contains around one hundred billion neurons and one hundred trillion synapses. Simple, right?

Given the New Testament's choice of analogies for the Church, should it come as any surprise that communication in the citywide Body of Christ is also intricately complicated? Communication breakdowns can be found in every marital failure or strain, and marital communication only involves two adult people who share daily common experiences. Families must learn to communicate, and those skills aren't simply acquired once but learned repeatedly at each new stage of development. Congregations combine all the complexities, histories, and brokenness of multiple family systems into one big communication conundrum— and the citywide Church tops it off by layering in differences in culture, ethnicity, leadership structures and expectations, and denominational distinctives in language, all resulting in never-ending spirals of complexity. Perhaps only spiritual brain surgeons need apply?

The organic side of the spectrum from the previous section might wish for all communication to come directly from the Head of the Body, Jesus. Through prayer, God will provide all the communication and coordination necessary for the body parts to align and collaborate. Obviously, prayer is an indispensable and foundational building block for citywide collaboration. If God isn't in it to both bless and inspire the work, no amount of human communication or coordination will produce anything worthy of the effort. On the other hand, the structured side might wish for something a little bit more concrete, recognizing that if it wouldn't work in a marriage for a husband and wife to rely solely on prayer, why would it work at infinitely more complicated levels in a city? Figuring out precisely how to effectively communicate within the entire Body of Christ in a city won't happen until sometime after Jesus returns. But the requirement to work at it and do our best, I'm convinced, is part of why Jesus' knees were so calloused.

WHEN WE COMMUNICATE IN A WAY THAT RECOGNIZES EVERY ROLE EVERY PART PLAYS, HUMBLE PRIDE IS THE RESULT.

It's ironic that the phase, "It's all Greek to me," has become a colloquial way of saying that communication has broken down and *no comprendo* whatever you're talking about. We don't have to choose between relying on spiritual communication through prayer and relying on human communication with one another. It's a both/and, not an either/or. In our communication with one another, we don't have to choose between impersonal forms of communication like letters and email or more personal forms like phone calls and face-to-face conversations. Both are necessary, and if cross cultural communication is the goal, becoming bilingual in communication styles is non-negotiable. We don't have to choose between communicating only with the leaders of an organization/church/nonprofit/business or the others in the entire group. We need to find ways to do both, which is particularly challenging and essential for citywide organizations like 4Tucson.

Fortunately, God is a colossal fan of communication. "In the beginning was the Word, and the Word was with God, and the Word was God." (John 1:1) Communication is God's very nature; the incarnation of Jesus is how God connected Himself to humanity in the ultimate form of Cross cultural communication. As challenging as communication can be, "If God is for us, who can be against us?" (Romans 8:31) Our ultra-relational God has shown us that, at the end of the day, it's all about relationships—and relationships of trust are how communication break-downs move from being breaking experiences to bonding ones through humble confession and forgiveness.

HUMBLE PRIDE

Tucson is unique with the presence of 4Tucson, designed to connect all the parts of the Body of Christ in the city and mobilize and prepare them to engage the culture at holistic, all-inclusive levels. This includes everything from prayer, worship, evangelism, and discipleship to working to see that all the domains, institutions, and policies of the city align with biblical principles. 4Tucson believes that a city that brings honor and glory to God will also provide tremendous opportunities and blessings for every person living within it.

The progress we've seen and cited in this book is tremendously encouraging. The strategic model noted in Chapter 6 has created momentum substantial in both its depth and breadth. Nobody on our staff could accurately describe everything that's already happening in the various domains, let alone articulate all of the possibilities on the horizon. The challenge comes in how to communicate excitement about this progress without it sounding like self-serving pride. The business domain brings with it expertise in areas like marketing, while the church and prayer domains are more at ease with humility. Like an alloy that combines two metals to make it stronger, if both perspectives can be combined, communication will be both stronger and more effective. Clear, consistent communication doesn't have to be the enemy of Spirit-led groundswells; surely there's a both/and that can be achieved somehow. Excitement and praise to God that invites others to get off the bench and into the game doesn't have to imply that our show is the only one in town. Partnering with 4Tucson and partnering with other churches and ministries are both/and, not either/or. Thankfully, 1 Corinthians 12 provides proper perspective. "If the foot should say, 'Because I am not a hand, I do not belong to the body,' it would not for that reason cease to be part of the body." (1 Corinthians 12:15) "The eye cannot say to the hand, 'I don't need you!'" (1 Corinthians 12:21) "If one part is honored, every part rejoices with it." (1 Corinthians 12:26) When we communicate in a way that recognizes every role every part plays, humble pride is the result. The tide can rise and bring every boat with it.

If the message is coming across as an either/or message (where one party celebrates at another party's expense) when a both/and message was intended, the problem is likely much deeper than a communication issue. Broken trust is the issue: either trust that was never formed out of relationships in the first place, or trust that somehow went sideways and now is mired in suspicion. People of the Cross have been given the ultimate tools for rebuilding trust. Broken trust is at its peak in peril when it's unrecognized. Reconciliation is not only possible but probable when individuals/groups speak the truth in love to one another, especially if both sides are significantly committed to one another, humble enough to each recognize and admit their own shortcomings, and in consistent communication with the healing Head of the Body.

> **DIVISION IS THE REALM OF THE ENEMY; UNITY/HARMONY IS CHARACTERISTIC OF THE SAVIOR.**

Becoming more Hebrew in our thinking is simply another way of following Jesus, who is simultaneously God and man, full of grace and truth, limitless in power and limitless in forgiveness. Division is the realm of the enemy; unity/harmony is characteristic of the Savior.

The final chapter ties together themes from throughout the book into seven bridge building tools that can help the City Church, the local congregation, and our own homes function in the unity/harmony for which Jesus prayed.

QUESTIONS FOR SELF-REFLECTION

- Where do you notice tendencies to create an either/or where God probably wants a both/and?

- Have you noticed when efforts in the Body of Christ jump straight to solutions without asking who else is already working in that area? What role can you play to be part of the solution instead of part of the problem?

- Do you tend toward the organic or the structured side of the continuum? Thank God right now for strengths and perspectives that you don't have. Is there someone you could also thank in person for working in ways unlike your own?

TODAY'S GPS

We praise You for Your Triune identity, perfectly combining Father, Son, and Holy Spirit such that who You are is love itself. We glorify You, Jesus, for the incarnation, for merging divinity with humanity in Your own body. We thank You for honoring God's law and Word without comparison, yet being known as a friend of sinners. Protect us from the enemy who seeks to divide what You intend to be held together. Show us how to pursue truth without unity/harmony being the victim, and how to excel at our unique positions within the Body of Christ while still honoring all the other parts of the same Body. Sanctify us by revealing areas where we're out of balance, and where we've mistakenly identified our piece as synonymous with the whole picture. Amen.

Chapter Nine

BRIDGE BUILDING TOOLS

U nity/harmony isn't easy. But it is an absolutely worthy endeavor, as Paul exhorts, "Make every effort to keep the unity of the Spirit through the bond of peace." (Ephesians 4:3) If achieving unity/ harmony was a deserving enough goal to cause our Lord and Savior, during His hour of greatest need, to labor in prayer over its fulfillment, we certainly will do well to join Him in praying that God work this unity/harmony in us—in our homes, our congregations, and our City Church. As the great preacher Charles Spurgeon said in reference to John 17, "This prayer is for you, and for me, as much as for the twelve apostles. May the Lord fulfill it in all of us as well as in them, for his dear name's sake! Amen."[1]

The most impressive physical bridges in the world span gaps that had been daunting for generations. Yet those chasms pale in comparison to the relational and ideological rifts all around us. When we look out at our conflicted world, it's easy to despair and wonder where on

---

1   Spurgeon's Verse Expositions of the Bible. http://www.studylight.org/commentaries/spe/ john-17.html

Earth we can start to make a significant difference. Thankfully, the Lord keeps revealing that it's not as complicated as we make it.

Over the last six years, the following seven tools have revealed themselves to be the key ingredients necessary to see Jesus' prayer answered at deeper levels in our cities, congregations, and homes. They also serve to pull together several of the themes covered throughout this book.

CONVICTION

When Mark Harris first met with me to explore the possibility of becoming 4Tucson's church domain director, one of my first convictions was to approach the position out of a model presented by Henry Blackaby. He wrote the influential book and series, *Experiencing God*, and the key point from that book is this: find where God is working and join Him in it rather than ask God to bless what you already plan to do. I said to Mark, "I have no intention of cold calling churches and trying to convince pastors who aren't already convinced. I don't see it as a good use of time to make a list of all the churches in the city and start systematically contacting them. I'd rather look for pastors who already have a Kingdom of God focus that's bigger than their own congregation and network/denomination. Are you cool with that?" Mark's answer was yes—and it was another confirmation that God was calling me to serve at 4Tucson.

IT TAKES CONVICTION TO WORK THROUGH CONFLICT RATHER THAN TO TAKE THE PATH OF LEAST RESISTANCE AND BAIL OUT.

My convictions about the strategic importance of unity/harmony grow daily. Not only is the concept what drove Jesus to His knees, it's a major theme throughout the entire New Testament. The unity/harmony presented in John 17 isn't an isolated teaching; it's thoroughly central to following Jesus. Bridge building will not happen in the Body of Christ without the conviction that bridge building is an indispensable part of following Jesus.

When a person is convicted that unity/harmony is not only strategic but faithful Christian living, they're also convinced that anything less is not only short-sighted but faithless and disobedient. When people or congregations realize that they are a vital part of the Body of Christ while always and forever only *one* part of the Body of Christ, they're determined to find ways to collaborate with *other* parts of the same Body regardless of the effort or time required. When we know from deep within us that others have perspectives, solutions, and wisdom that we need (and vice versa), we'll actively look for ways to build relationships beyond our comfort zones. The first hurdles might trip us up, but they won't stop us. We won't settle on waiting for opportunities to come; we'll actively pursue those opportunities and take advantage of them when they are there.

When I wrote *Jesus' Surprising Strategy,* I titled Chapter 3, "Investing or Cheering?" There's a huge difference between being a fan of unity/harmony and an investor in it. What I've learned since writing that book is that the difference is more critical than I first believed. Why? It takes conviction to work through conflict rather than to take the path of least resistance and bail out. It takes perseverance to rub shoulders with others where the only thing you have in common is Jesus. It takes humility to grow and mature once you notice each other's blind spots and start to address them. And it takes "a long obedience in the same direction"[2] for the unity/harmony we achieve to be visible enough and awe-inspiring enough for the world to come to know the love of God and the identity of Jesus. If it was easy, Jesus wouldn't have prayed for it.

HUMILITY

In one of my early planning sessions for this book, I considered ending every chapter with some aspect of humility. If it's not the most important characteristic of investors in unity/harmony, it's second only to

---

2   Title of a book written by Eugene Peterson.

conviction. Unity/harmony won't likely be pursued at all without significant humility—and it is certain unity/harmony won't survive through the trials and conflicts without humility.

We never get to graduate from humility. Death to self is a daily process.[3] We can't learn all future life lessons in the present season or chapter of our lives, and the way we die to ourselves today will look differently than the way God will call us to die to ourselves next year. Each day will bring opportunities, and the next day will present new ones. Humility happens when we recognize the size of the challenge, realize that it's impossible to do anything about it apart from God, and express trust and confidence in God's character to face the challenge. God regularly and intentionally brings us to the end of ourselves.

> **WE NEVER GET TO GRADUATE FROM HUMILITY. DEATH TO SELF IS A DAILY PROCESS.**

Patrick Lencioni, best-selling author and popular speaker in the field of business management, has been a regular faculty member of the Willow Creek Global Leadership Summits. In 2016, he shared the back story of writing the book, *The Ideal Team Player*. He had long ago identified three core values/virtues to identifying potential employees, but had never written them up because he didn't think they were that insightful. After multiple requests over many years, he finally put them into a book—and was shocked at how strong and positive the response was to the principles. What is the first core value/virtue he seeks? Humility. At that same summit, Bill Hybels shared again, "The world is desperate to find leaders who will put others' needs ahead of their own. The highest value at the Global Leadership Summit is leadership. Armed with enough humility, we can learn from anyone."

Do we want to prepare the way for the King of kings to enter our city and reign? Then we must have the attitude of John the Baptist, who said

---

3   Luke 9:23: "Whoever wants to be my disciple must deny themselves and take up their cross daily and follow me."

about Jesus, "I am filled with joy at his success. [30]He must become greater and greater, and I must become less and less." (John 3:29–30, NLT) This attitude toward other leaders will smooth out the rough places, level the hills of pride, and fill in the valleys caused by envy. Matthew 12:25 (NLT) says, "Any kingdom divided by civil war is doomed. A town or family splintered by feuding will fall apart." Humility is the glue that holds relationships together.

I came across this litany/prayer written by Rafael Cardinal Merry del Val (1865–1930), Secretary of State for Pope Saint Pius X, that reflects on Jesus and exquisitely captures the heart of humility:

> O Jesus! meek and humble of heart, Hear me.
> From the desire of being esteemed,
> Deliver me, Jesus.
> From the desire of being loved...
> From the desire of being extolled...
> From the desire of being honored...
> From the desire of being praised...
> From the desire of being preferred to others...
> From the desire of being consulted...
> From the desire of being approved...
> From the fear of being humiliated...
> From the fear of being despised...
> From the fear of suffering rebukes...
> From the fear of being calumniated...
> From the fear of being forgotten...
> From the fear of being ridiculed...
> From the fear of being wronged...
> From the fear of being suspected...
> That others may be loved more than I,
> Jesus, grant me the grace to desire it.
> That others may be esteemed more than I...
> That, in the opinion of the world,
> others may increase and I may decrease...
> That others may be chosen and I set aside...

That others may be praised and I unnoticed...
That others may be preferred to me in everything...
That others may become holier than I,
    provided that I may become as holy as I should...

TRANSPARENCY

Transparency is one of the key ways humility manifests itself. Transparency helps level the playing field and disarms some of the enemy's chief tools of pride, jealousy, and envy when building relationships with those who are very different from us, or with whom trust has been broken or never successfully built.

Transparency is best illustrated by its opposite. Has this ever happened to you? The Good Book says not to let the sun go down on your anger, but one Saturday night, you and your spouse decide to make an exception. Sunday morning rolls around after a restless night of non-sleep, and you get up to find that the coffeemaker picked today to roll over and play dead. The dog also tore up the living room sofa during the night, and the cat deposited hairballs for you to step in as you trod into the living room. When you wake up the kids, they're grumpy and ask why they have to go to church, even though it's been the same routine every Sunday of their lives. By the time you pile in the car, everyone is late and screams of "Stop touching

IF WE CAN'T BE REAL WITH ONE ANOTHER IN THE BODY OF CHRIST, SOMETHING IS SERIOUSLY AMISS.

me!" echo from the kids in the back seat. The car screeches into the church parking lot well after the start of the service, everyone slams their door before marching up to the foyer, and a friendly usher greets you at the door. "Good morning!" he says with a beaming smile. "How are you doing this blessed day?" To which you reply... "Fine, thanks."

Transparency doesn't imply that you must dump the entire load on the unsuspecting usher. But hopefully, in a congregation full of Christ followers, at least *sometime* during the morning you can be real enough with someone to share how you really felt—or even address bigger concerns: "I just had to put my parents in a nursing home," or, "My child just announced he's no longer a believer," or "My wife was diagnosed with cancer," or "It looks like I could lose my job this week." If we can't be real with one another in the Body of Christ, something is seriously amiss.

In our Pastors Partnership group, we didn't begin with a well-established foundation of trust. There was more suspicion coming into the room than anticipation. But it was transparency that changed the tenor of the meetings; that, and a conviction that Jesus is praying that we learn how to love one another. As person after person shared their stories, revealed their brokenness, and tore off their masks over the following weeks, authentic relationships were developed. Love for one another is much more likely between real people than between mannequins.

Leaders can model transparency, but in any small group it only takes one brave soul to change the group dynamic by taking a risk and being transparent. Transparency also prevents posturing between leaders of different congregations, sectors, or organizations. And the query, "Can you pray for me?" can break the ice in any tension-filled environment when it's sincere, heartfelt, and personal.

Mike Hildebrandt, a Tucson staff member for the Navigators, shared during a recent sermon that one of their goals for the coming year was to minister out of their brokenness. What a wise goal, especially for campus ministries! The younger a person is, the quicker they are to sniff out hypocrisy. Transparency is so much more attractive than play acting! Christians experience bumps and bruises just like everyone else, and until we face them and work through them in the Body of Christ, we're likely to transfer those wounds to others. As the saying goes, hurt people hurt people. Transparency not only helps us as we process challenges, it gives permission for everyone else to do the same.

LISTENING

Like the first level of unity from *Jesus' Surprising Strategy,* "Common Kindness," listening seems so simple—yet people are so desperate for someone to listen to them they'll even pay complete strangers like counselors for the privilege. One simple phrase that I first mentioned in Chapter 4 has proven golden in bridge building between diverse people: "Help me understand." In our Pastors Partnership group, executing this phrase enabled us to successfully navigate the shark-infested waters of politics with love and mutual respect. "Help me understand" is the polar opposite of "Here's why I'm right." "Help me understand" is also the olive branch that can end a battle just as effectively as preventing one. Can you imagine how many bridges burned could've been saved from destruction by a genuine desire to listen and understand? In any context (City Church, congregation, home) and at any time (relationship building, pre-conflict, mid-conflict, post-conflict), listening is a bridge building tool that honors and values the other party. "Help me understand" is a practical way that Paul's "Body of Christ" analogy for the City Church gets operationalized, because it starts from the premise that every part of the Body is valuable and brings gifts that we don't have by ourselves.

> ## "HELP ME UNDERSTAND" IS THE POLAR OPPOSITE OF "HERE'S WHY I'M RIGHT."

4Tucson's Mark Harris tells a story from his Baptist seminary days of being given a class assignment to visit denominations quite different from his own for a Sunday worship service. Because his professor had taught his students to ask, "Help me understand," the assignment was a beneficial bridge-building experience for Mark. Instead of the assignment being a compare and contrast exercise where any less-than-Baptist "shortcomings" were identified, Mark discovered that Jesus was the common thread in all of the worship services he attended. No wonder Mark is now working to unite the many flavors of Christians in Tucson.

In my hundreds of pre-marriage counseling sessions, my top guideline for the couples in their communication with each other was, "Be a ready listener and don't interrupt." I also tell couples that communication is learned; we enter with nothing, and learn every good and bad communication habit we have—which means we can all learn to step up our game in the skill of listening. Listening is not waiting until the other person comes up for air so that you can launch your well-prepared rebuttal. Skilled listening works to be effective at understanding what the other person *meant* even if it's not what they *said*. In fact, advanced listening is being able to identify the emotions behind the words, and helping the other person discover things about themselves they never realized before.

Dennis Watson has been my life coach for five years, and I've often wondered how much more effective I would have been as a congregational pastor if I'd accessed his guidance all those years ago. His primary contribution to 4Tucson is coaching any staff who are interested, and I can't imagine a greater contribution than that. Dennis is a world-class listener who regularly says, "I don't have the answers; you do. My job is to help you discover what God's already placed inside of you."

In any context and at any time, listening is a bridge building tool that honors and values the other party. Skilled listening can synchronize relationships like few other tools.

THANKSGIVING

Much has been written about the indispensable role of thanksgiving in the Christian life. A thankful heart is a healthy heart. C.S. Lewis wrote, "Praise is inner health made audible."[4] Even more, "Enter his gates with thanksgiving and his courts with praise" (Psalm 100:4) suggests that thanksgiving is how we enter God's presence, the very way we begin to commune with God.

Thanksgiving is just as vital in communing with other people. Creating a "culture of honor" will go a long way toward building unity/harmony in the City Church. Pastor Angel Morfin teaches, "When we

---

4   *Reflections on the Psalms*, p. 94.

encourage each other and build each other up, the spirit of competition is broken." Barnabas played a significant role in the life of the early Church, and Acts 4:36 tells us that Barnabas wasn't his given name; it was Joseph. Barnabas was a nickname given to him by the apostles that meant, "Son of Encouragement." Paul might never have been accepted by the other apostles, much less had the impact he did on Christianity, if not for Barnabas' partnership, encouragement, and thanksgiving for the work of God in Paul's life. If John Mark is the author of the gospel of Mark, as many conclude, Barnabas played a pivotal role in yet another New Testament book. Barnabas was the one who included John Mark when others, including Paul, wanted to give up on him after his failure on a previous mission trip. In its sidebar on Barnabas, the Life Application Bible notes, "It is delightful that wherever Barnabas encouraged Christians, non-Christians flocked to become believers."

> A CULTURE OF HONOR PRAISES GOD WHILE THANKING OTHERS.

Greg Ayers, founder of GAP Ministries in Tucson, has created a culture of honor within GAP that also extends to other ministries in the city. One year 4Tucson unexpectedly received a huge gift basket personally delivered from GAP simply as an expression of their thanksgiving. This act of kindness and thanksgiving inspired us to start implementing some "culture of honor" traditions within our organization as well. One example is a card signed by every 4Tucson staff member every week for the lead pastor of the "Church of the Week." Each week, over 100 churches in our city pray for the "Church of the Week," which is recognized with a brief description, thanksgiving to God, and a prayer request from the congregation. The card is handcrafted by a group of stampers from a local church, and accompanied by a gift as an expression of thanks. Another example is a "City Changer of the Week" card that honors someone well known or little known whose service in our city is making a difference. Each 4Tucson staff member writes a personal note of encouragement and together we pray for the honoree.

Romans 12 is another John 17 chapter reflecting Jesus' prayer at multiple points. Verses 9–11 reference the "culture of honor" tool as central to fulfilling Jesus' command to love one another. "Don't just pretend to love others. Really love them. Hate what is wrong. Hold tightly to what is good. ¹⁰Love each other with genuine affection, and take delight in honoring each other. ¹¹Never be lazy, but work hard and serve the Lord enthusiastically." (Romans 12:9–11, NLT) Take delight in honoring each other because it's a key way to align ourselves with Jesus' heartbeat in John 17.

The "missing middle" section of the last chapter is one more example of living out a culture of honor. When we set out to solve problems all by ourselves, we miss out on opportunities to honor others whom God may have similarly called. But when we join hands and say, "How can we help?" we bestow incredible honor on God's work in another's life. Few activities I know of have done more to create new bridges of trust than simply joining, supporting, and celebrating something somebody else started. A culture of honor praises God while thanking others, and the "inner health made audible" improves the health of the whole City Church.

SERVICE

Service is the sweet spot everyone understands. If we want our unity/harmony to be visible to the watching world, serving together is one of the most effective ways of achieving that goal. Service is at the heart of the church-school partnerships and church-foster care partnerships that have opened such tremendous doors in Tucson and other cities around the country. "How can we pray for you?" and "How can we help?" are questions that are almost always met with appreciation. All of the astounding opportunities God is giving us at 4Tucson have service somewhere in their development.

RuthAnn Smithrud is the local outreach director for St. Andrew's Presbyterian Church in Tucson, one of many churches in our city with a tremendous heart for service. RuthAnn is responsible for coordinating St. Andrew's "Service Worship" once a quarter. On the fifth Sundays of the month, instead of the congregation gathering internally for worship, they're commissioned to go throughout the city to serve. Other congregations in town have joined this practice because of its impact in revealing the love of God to love-starved members of our community.

Mike Birrer is another servant leader in our city. Mike founded Serve Tucson and is a phenomenal networker, bringing together college students, refugees, school communities, cyclists, Christmas carolers, and anyone else in the community with a heart for the city. After three years of praying around the city, he felt God's nudge to bring people together to clean up some of the messes and restore Tucson's natural beauty. He's always got a rake or hoe in his hand and is busy beautifying a vacant lot or a street corner. His service warranted a feature article in our city's main newspaper, as well as a $5,000 award by a local business, which he used to buy more tools to enable more servants.

SERVICE IS THE SWEET SPOT EVERYONE UNDERSTANDS.

Lisa Chastain is the founder of Hope Network which hosts the annual Tucson HopeFest, probably the largest collaborative service effort in the city. Each fall tens of thousands of people gather at Kino Stadium to receive food, clothing, haircuts, connections to needed social services, dental work—and as much love and prayer as they can handle. Lisa does a remarkable job of partnering with the business and government communities while maintaining the Christ-centered identity of the event. She coined the phrase "collaboration without compromise" to describe her process of building partnerships of service that bless and benefit thousands of people throughout Southern Arizona.

Service is enormously effective in building bridges into the community—but it's just as successful in building bridges to one another. Another servant-hearted church in our city annually signs up for cleanup duty after the citywide Worship Over Tucson service in an outdoor park. This annual event is a Cross culture experience instituted and led by believers from one ethnicity, with the group signing up to serve a different ethnicity, and the simple behind-the-scenes act of picking up trash after the service speaks volumes about Jesus' prayer to love one another until the world notices.

PRAYER

Where else can we end but where we began—with prayer? If it was easy, Jesus wouldn't have prayed for it. Since He did, we can surmise that prayer itself can be a powerful bridge building tool of its own. When we hear a brother or sister in Christ cry out to God for similar desires as our own, our hearts are immediately knit together. The fact that they might pray using different words, styles, or patterns doesn't matter. I'm filled with gratitude every time I hear fellow Tucsonans praying to and praising God in different languages even when I know few or none of the words they're saying.

Prayer aligns our hearts with God's heart. Jeremiah 29:7 says, "Also, seek the peace and prosperity of the city to which I have carried you into exile. Pray to the Lord for it, because if it prospers, you too will prosper." We may not yet have a heart for our city, but if we pray as Jesus prayed, we can develop one. When we both pray for our city leaders and develop relationships with them, not only do the relationships enrich the prayers, but the prayers deepen the relationships. Prayer gives us the conviction we need to break the deadly spirits of competition and apathy.

One of 4Tucson's first printed materials was the Pray4Tucson prayer bookmark that features different petitions designed to turn our hearts toward our city, toward God, and toward one another. We don't know how many hundreds or thousands of people are praying these prayers each day, but we give out the bookmarks whenever we can and pray the number continues to grow. Here's what the bookmark says:

- *Sunday:* Pray for unity in the Body of Christ (John 17:21, 23)

- *Monday:* Pray for God to bless and prosper our city (Jeremiah 29:7)

- *Tuesday:* Pray for God to replace ungodly leadership with godly leadership (Daniel 2:21 and Romans 13:1)

- *Wednesday:* Pray for God to send more workers into the harvest (Matthew 9:36–38)

- *Thursday:* Pray for growing partnership between schools and congregations (Matthew 5:16)

- *Friday:* Pray that our city would not give in to a spirit of poverty (Ephesians 3:19–20)

- *Saturday:* Pray for healthy families in Tucson (Deuteronomy 6:6, 31:12)

Worship leaders from different congregations have gathered together, prayed, worshiped, made music together, and written new songs that are prayers for our city. Two City Psalms albums have been released so far with more in the works, and some of these songs are now heard in citywide gatherings and in local congregations. I regularly tell people that dodging the city's infamous road potholes is now enjoyable with my City Psalms CDs accompanying the drive. God is writing a new song in and for our city!

> PRAYER GIVES US THE CONVICTION WE NEED TO BREAK THE DEADLY SPIRITS OF COMPETITION AND APATHY.

Jesus was intentional about what He prayed on Good Friday Eve. If we will be as intentional as He is, we can build bridges that will bring honor and glory to Jesus while blessing our friends and neighbors with greater knowledge of God and His love. Tools, no matter how powerful, accomplish nothing until they're put to use.

QUESTIONS FOR SELF-REFLECTION

- Which of these seven bridge building tools do you most regularly use? Which are least familiar to you?

- Think of people you consider to be bridge builders. Which tools do they use?

- What new steps from this chapter do you want to take to become an answer to Jesus' prayer for your city, congregation, and home?

- What new steps from this book do you want to take to become an answer to Jesus' prayer for your city, congregation, and home?

TODAY'S GPS

Our Father in Heaven, thank You for being a bridge building God by releasing Your Son Jesus to take on human flesh. Your love for humankind is limitless, sparing no expense in bridging the eternal gap between You and Your children. Jesus, we honor You, we praise You, and we glorify You for being that bridge at unfathomable personal cost. We invite You—we need You—to become more preeminent in our thoughts, our values, our priorities, and our relationships. Like John the Baptist, we pray that You may become greater and greater, while we become less and less. Protect us from the enemy who seeks to distract us from the hard work of bridge building, and who seeks to encourage us to engage in the destructive work of bridge burning. Sanctify us to become more and more like You, leaving the safety of heavenly places to build bridges into a dangerous and divided world. We are so honored that You invite us into this powerful, creative, redemptive adventure. Thank You, thank You, thank You. Amen.

ROSE TEDEROUS' TESTIMONY: JULY 2016

S o my story begins like this. Actually, it begins way back when, but I gotta start somewhere.

Summer of 2016 heated up: yes by temperature but mostly I'm talking about the racial tension in the country. I knew I was becoming more and more outside myself and my body. I regularly tried to get a white friend into a serious dialogue on Facebook, and spent hours in conversation expressing my views and feelings, which were mostly unpopular to this white person. I knew I was outside myself after these long, drawn out conversations, when I would repost something to help make my point. I wanted you to understand, white person, that Black Lives Matter was really about black lives matter. I was exhausted in trying to convince others that black lives matter. I would not hear anything that would shut the conversation down about how all lives matter; you know, like my Christian brothers and sisters saying, "But Jesus died for all of us, so you see, Rose, we are all the same. Jesus does not see color..."

What I heard was, "Jesus loves all of us the same, so you see, racism does not matter or even exist. Therefore, the brutal murder at the hands of police of those black men and all the other murders by police do not matter because God loves us all." What I also heard—again, remember, this is not what was actually said—"So there, case closed, no need for drawn out conversations on race issues again." Then there was, "But Rose, all lives matter. Come on. How can you just say black lives matter when all lives matter?" This one bothered me so bad. Of course, I found all kinds of posts that tried to explain why the Black Lives Matter movement even existed. To me, saying all lives matter was really just trying to shut down all conversation about racial issues. I was exhausted.

This was just Facebook; then there was the TV media. When I watched the video of those two black men gunned down, as I see it, by police, it was like in my brain yelling, "See, ALL LIVES DON'T MATTER!" I was obsessed. I stayed up sometimes all night watching this on TV, and in between I would be on my phone and on Facebook. I was being drawn into complete and utter darkness. I could not help it.

Of course, my Jesus is so great. He kept His hand on me; it was like Jesus was pulling my arm one way while I was pulling the other way. Let me explain. During this time, it was really a span of about three weeks, I was still doing my spiritual work kinda sort of ... well, actually, the side God was pulling was doing spiritual work. I still got up in the mornings first thing with my Bible and daily reader. But as things heated up with the shootings, then the police being killed in Dallas, I was really beside myself. You see, it's not so much that what I was feeling and going through was wrong, or that none of this was happening, or that I was making up stuff and pulling the race card. This was as real to me as breathing air; this was as real in this country as needing fuel for our bodies; this racism is as real as the need that I have for a Jesus to save us "yesterday." So, yes, I was not wrong in what I was going through—but it was becoming my god. I was worshiping this battle against darkness in this country. I was being fed but not getting full, so I kept glued to it, wanting satisfaction, wanting resolution, wanting accountability, wanting my parched thirst for equality to be relieved. I was not angry anymore. I was beyond that. I was numb, disappointed, scared, frustrated. I felt I had no place for this fast-flowing current coursing through my body, the uncontained energy called adrenaline.

So I used Facebook, plus my family talking for hours on the issues of historical racism, the evilness of how this country came about, the genocide of Native Americans and the enslavement of African-American people, all done at the hands of the white man. I talked to anyone who gave me the slightest inkling that they would listen. I needed people to understand because the white man has not made amends for evil he created, this is what we get. The white man is reaping what he sowed.

Finally, I hear of a Black Lives Matter rally and vigil honoring the latest victims of police brutality. I feel myself relax; finally, a place to go to relieve myself of this anxiety, a place to say out loud, BLACK LIVES MATTER. But before I go on, let me explain something to those of you thinking I must be the racist. Because that is now the new way of cutting the conversation off: accuse the victim of wrongdoing; blame the victim. Of course, those in power and control have always been good at that.

I mentioned that this was over a three-week period. Also during this time, while I was going through this craziness about racism, a dear friend of mine was dying. This friend is a white woman. I mention that only for the sake of this conversation, because for me when I went to the hospital and hugged her, kissed her, and held her hand, she was just my friend. Once she was out of the hospital, when me and a couple of other girlfriends (white friends) went to visit her in her home, I kicked her son out of the room and I crawled onto that king-size waterbed and held her hands, hugged her fragile body, and the only thing I saw was my friend, not her color. Or when I went alone to see her on Sunday morning instead of church, this was my church, taking her a kale smoothie, lying in her waterbed sharing stories, rubbing her arms, holding her hands and hugging her. I only saw my friend. Then the last Sunday that I was alone with her giving her the *Jesus Calling* daily reader and reading Scripture to her, praying with her and her husband, all while lying beside this beautiful dying friend of mine, I saw only my friend. Not once did either of us *not* see our colors, our differences. We knew and we were okay. The last Sunday I saw her alive was on the day before her birthday. Her wonderful husband gave her a birthday party. I did go to church with my grandchildren on this day, and afterwards took them to the party with me. Not once especially during this time of the heat of the racial tension was I not aware of being black, and the possibilities of going to this party where more than likely I would be the only African-American. I was the only African-American, with the exception of my mixed beauties, my grandbabies. I got to see my friend and for the last time climbed in that waterbed, held her around the waist, our heads against each other, and just lavished in our love and friendship. The party was great, with lots of love and family and friends there to share their love. But I must say, as I was outside watching my grandbabies swim, there were several men outside as well. I kept praying, "Lord, please don't let them bring up the racial stuff." I later thought how obsessed I was to even think these people would be thinking about what's going on outside these walls with their beloved mother, wife, friend, colleague, sister, aunt, and grandmother dying in the next room.

So I tell you—this is what was happening during the heat of the racial tension in July 2016.

And now for Grace and "I matter." In March of 2016, I signed up to attend a women's spiritual retreat called John 17. I really had not thought much of it until it was confirmed I was chosen to attend. My spiritual sponsor called to let me know she would pick me up and bring me home. She also reminded me I could not bring a watch or my cell phone. I also received an email on what items to bring. Because I knew very little about this retreat, I'll admit it went through my mind the whole "Kool Aide thing;" yes, Jim Jones and that cult from years ago. But I said to myself, it's not that far from home and the three-day retreat is held at the church I often attend. Also, I trust my God. But I also felt reluctant. It crossed my mind to cancel. With all the racial tension, I just did not want to be the only African-American woman in a room full of white folks I didn't know; didn't know their political views; didn't know how angry they were about the police in Dallas murdered by a black man. I just didn't want to deal with any of it. But God knows so much more than me: imagine that.

So on Thursday, July 14, I get up and proceed to do hours of yard work. Now I'm sore and can barely move, thinking, "This could be a good reason to cancel!" Yeah, right. I spend a few hours resting my body and, of course, realize, "I've not packed for the retreat for which my spiritual sponsor will pick me up in a couple of hours." I get up and throw a few outfits in a suitcase, take my shower, gather a sleeping bag and air mattress, and have 45 minutes before I am to leave. I check my cell phone. My dear friend had passed away. I received a text from her husband. My heart is breaking; I'm almost shocked although we all knew it would not be long. All I could say out loud was, "Oh no, oh no." I called her husband and offered my condolences, all the while holding back my tears. My heart broke from just imagining what he must be going through. I then called a mutual friend. I contemplated not going to the retreat. I thought there is no way I would miss the chance to say my final goodbyes. The other issue was that I understood that I was not supposed to have my cell phone, and how could anyone get in touch with me?

Okay, so now I have a real excuse not to go, right God? Yeah right. You see, we had been provided with an emergency phone number to leave at home so our loved ones could reach us if need be. So I gave my mutual friend my home number (yes, we still have a landline) and begged her to call and let my husband know about the funeral services. He could then call the emergency number. Well, it seems if not even someone's death could keep me away, then this spiritual women's retreat was meant to be. In fact, after all the excuses—the death of my dear friend, the racial tension, and my obsession over it, God had this planned anyway. God knew exactly where I needed to be.

Ten minutes before 5:00 p.m., my spiritual sponsor came. I had never met her. Tell me why she was the perfect sponsor for me. Good job, God. Here I am, this completely exhausted, broken, grieving woman saying,

"Here you go, Lord. Take me as I am." We arrive at the church where the retreat is to be held. From the moment we pulled into the parking lot, I was to do nothing and was there only to be served by Christ through the people who committed themselves to us for the weekend. Remember, I went to this retreat in grief from the loss of my friend, which I only heard about one hour earlier, and with racial tension, frustration, anger, and the Black Lives Matter mantra. But when I walked through the doors to the registration table with my spiritual sponsor beside me, something changed. I felt peace from the moment I was greeted. I felt the presence of Christ. I saw the hands and feet of God. There were speakers, surprises, good food, singing, praise and worship, group work, holy communion every day, and lots and lots of hugs and tears.

But most of all, I began to deal with "I don't matter" directly linked to Black Lives Matter. For the first time in my life, I understood grace and the cross, and when someone said, as if Christ was speaking, "I did it for you," I fully and totally understood how much I matter; how much Christ gave me grace. I also understand that the Black Lives Matter movement is linked, I would suspect, to the feeling that as African-Americans historically and now with what is going on with the racial issues, I am not the only one that personally feels that he/she doesn't matter. Racism and oppression are real, with the continued obvious inequalities of African-American people and people of color in this country. But what I know without a doubt is that I matter. I matter to God; He gives me grace every day. Through the hands and feet of Christ at this retreat, and through the many surprises, each *agape* said loud and clear, "You matter to me, Rose," signed, Jesus, by His blood.

Because I matter to Jesus, I now feel the strength to fight injustice as a whole person, not as a broken person. With this knowledge and Jesus as my guide, I can fight injustice with love.

CITY TRANSFORMATION TRAINING OVERVIEW

by
DR. TONY SIMMS
4Tucson Chief Operating Officer and Vice President
of the Domains and Taskforces Division

ere is a picture of Jerusalem during Nehemiah's time:

1 Upper house of the king
2 House of Azaraiah
3 House of Benjamin and Hasshub
4 House of Eliashib the high priest
5 Ascent to the armoury
6 House of the mighty men
7 Artificial pool
8 Sepulchres of David

A Upper chamber of the corner
B House of the temple servants
and the merchants
C Chamber of Meshullam son of Berechiah
D House of Zadok son of Immer
E Houses of the priests
F House of Jedaiah
son of Harumaph

Present wall
of Old City

Tower of Hananel
Tower of the Hundred
Sheep Gate
Fish Gate
Old Gate
Muster Gate
East Gate
Horse Gate
Broad Wall
Ophel
Tower of the Ovens
Great projecting tower
Valley Gate
Older wall
Projecting tower
Water Gate
Projecting tower
Fountain Gate
Dung Gate
Stairs descending
from City of David

Jerusalem had a variety of issues that functioned as challenges to City Transformation:

- Jerusalem's city walls were broken down; therefore, it was unable to protect itself (Nehemiah 1:3)

- According to Kidner, "[Jerusalem's] most likely background is the sequence in Ezra 4:7–23, in which a bid to rebuild the walls had been reported to king Artaxerxes and promptly crushed 'by force and power.' It was an ominous development, for the ring of hostile neighbours around Jerusalem could now claim royal backing."[1]

- Jerusalem was unable to be a distinctive Jewish city with godly customs and traditions (Nehemiah 1:3)

- The newly rebuilt temple was exposed to the danger of being attacked again (Nehemiah 1:3)

- The people of Jerusalem were not able to advance the cause and glory of God (Nehemiah 1:4)

- There existed a failure of the people to refrain from corruption and keep God's commandments (Nehemiah 1:4–7)

- Desolate tombs represented hopelessness due to the lack of family and historical legacy (Nehemiah 2:3)

- Burned gates represented a loss of social life (community); people were afraid to engage in social interactions (Nehemiah 2:3)

- The Jews were in bondage and were powerless to change their circumstances due to their lack of autonomy and authority (Nehemiah 2:7–8)

---

1   Kidner, D. (1979), *Ezra & Nehemiah: An Introduction & Commentary*, p. 78, InterVarsity Press, Downers Grove, Ill.

- The Jews lacked the financial capacity to secure the necessary resources to rebuild the wall (Nehemiah 2:7–8)

- The Jews lacked the military might necessary to overcome opposition (Nehemiah 2:9–10)

- Enemies of the Jews were working to thwart all efforts of rebuilding Jerusalem (Nehemiah 2:10)

- The Jews were seen as insignificant (to daily life) by those living in the surrounding communities (Nehemiah 4:7–8)

According to Douglas and Tenney, "Nehemiah's great work of restoring the wall of Jerusalem depended basically on securing permission from the king (Artaxerxes) . . . [Ezra] had been hindered in his work by adverse royal decrees secured by his enemies."[2]

JERUSALEM'S CITY TRANSFORMATION STRATEGY

GOALS

- Gain permission and authority to return to Jerusalem to rebuild the city's walls (Nehemiah 2:2–7).

- Secure resources to rebuild the city's walls (Nehemiah 2:8).

- Inspire and mobilize Jerusalem's people to rebuild the city's walls (Nehemiah 2:17–19).

- Restore godliness to the city of Jerusalem (Nehemiah 5:1–13).

OUTPUTS

- *Conveners, Leaders, Craftsmen and Builders*—men led their families, brothers, and households to rebuild specific areas of the city's walls (Nehemiah 3:1–32).

---

2   Douglas, J.D., & Tenney M.C., (1987), *The New International Dictionary of the Bible*, p. 970, The Zondervan Corporation.

- *Protectors*—the Jews setup protection to guard the rebuilding project day and night (Nehemiah 4:9–23).

- *Repentance*—the people of Jerusalem repented of their sins and sought after God (Nehemiah 5:12–13).

OUTCOMES

The rebuilding of these 16-plus areas of the city's walls would restore the Jews' psychological, emotional, physical, and spiritual well-being concerning their relationship with God.

- Sheep Gate
- Tower of the Hundred
- Tower of Hananel
- Fish Gate
- Old Gate
- Broad Wall
- Tower of Furnaces (Ovens)
- Valley Gate
- Refuse (Dung) Gate
- Fountain Gate
- Projecting Tower (upper house)
- Water Gate
- Great Projecting Tower
- Horse Gate
- East Gate
- Inspection Gate

JERUSALEM'S CITY TRANSFORMATION METHODS

- *Awareness of Issues/Challenges*—Information about issues/challenges was collected from trusted sources (Nehemiah 1:1–3).

- *Seeking God*—Nehemiah immediately recognized his frailty and instantly sought God on these issues/challenges (Nehemiah 1:4–6).

- *Repentance Before God*—Nehemiah began asking God for forgiveness for the Jews and himself (Nehemiah 1:6–7).

- *Restoration and Favor from God*—Nehemiah began asking God to restore Israel for God's and the Jew's sake (Nehemiah 1:8–11).

- *Understanding and Submitting to God's Authority (and those with authority)*—Nehemiah understood that he was under the authority of the King of Persia (Artaxerxes) and that he was first and foremost subject to the wishes of the King. Therefore, before he could accomplish what he asked God for, he needed to navigate God's structured authority by informing the king of the issues/challenges, then making a request to act upon his plan to address those issues (Nehemiah 2:1–6).

- *Asking Those in Authority for Assistance*—Nehemiah recognized the hand of God moving in his interactions with the King of Persia. He understood that God had given him favor with the king. Therefore, Nehemiah did not stop with asking for permission to solve the issues/challenges, he asked the king to participate in solving the issues/challenges by supplying needed authority, resources, and military assistance (Nehemiah 2:6–8).

- *Surveying and Analyzing the City's Issues/Challenges*—Nehemiah understood the importance of gaining a full understanding of the issues/challenges first hand. He understood that being intimate with the issues/challenges before discussing them with others was prudent and enabled him to speak with authority and clarity (Nehemiah 2:9–15).

- *Meeting with Jerusalem's City Leaders*—Nehemiah understood that to rebuild the city's walls required the participation of many people. Those people would include: public leaders (officials), religious leaders (priests), people of influence (nobles), conveners, and workers (Nehemiah 2:16).

- *Inspiring People to Participate in Solving Issues/Challenges and Executing the Plan*—It was not enough for Nehemiah to simply state facts; he needed to inspire his peers to act with conviction, the type of conviction that would overcome future discouragement and resentments (Nehemiah 2:17–18).

- *Understanding the Complexities of an Environment (autonomy, authority, capacity, etc.)*—Public officials from other towns/cities were in opposition to the rebuilding of Jerusalem. Sanballat (Governor of Samaria), Tobiah (Governor of Ammon), and Geshem (Chief of the Arabs) did not want the Jews (God) to exist in the area (Nehemiah 2:19).

- *Seeking God and Learning how to Respond to Opposition*—Nehemiah refused to act in his own strength to address the opposition. He immediately referenced God as the one in whom the opposition would have to contend based on what He (God) desired for the area (Nehemiah 2:20; 4:1–23; 6:1–14).

TUCSON'S ISSUES AND CHALLENGES TO CITY TRANSFORMATION

- A low percentage of Christian businesses are effectively equipped to deliver quality products and services

- Christian business owners need support

- Tucson ranks in the Top 10 most "unchurched" cities in the nation (less than 10 percent of city residents attending a Christian church on any given week)[3]

- Christian congregations and organizations have historically been isolated from one another, especially denominationally and ethnically, and therefore not working together to solve city issues

---

3   Barna, http://cities.barna.org/barna-cities-the-top-churchless-metro-areas/

- Even among congregations that have committed to work together, a low percentage of individual Christians know how to work with other Christians outside their own congregation to solve city issues

- A low percentage of churches and schools working together

- A low percentage of seniors graduating from high school

- A high percentage of single family households with limited access to healthy role models and mentors

- A high number of high school graduates not attending college or dropping out of college

- A low percentage of parental engagement throughout students' entire school experience

- Tucson has a high percentage of unchurched residents, therefore, decisions concerning natural resources are often made that are neither good for the people (living in the area) or for the stewardship of the natural resources

- Families and children need clean parks where they can play

- Godly solutions in the public square depend on Christians having the ability to collaborate with and influence state legislators

- Society has a growing level of resistance to authority, the rulers which God has put in place

- The American form of government requires an informed and submitted electorate (people) who understand its constitution

- Governments, if unchecked, can abuse their power and their citizens

- Due to the rising costs of health care, it is important for individuals to take personal responsibility for their own health and quality of life

- Over the last 20 years, Americans have struggled with obesity

- There are a low number of Christian healthcare agencies working together to address city resident's physical and mental health issues

- To encourage mental health, citizens should enjoy God's creation, fellowshipping with other Jesus followers, having a better outlook on life, and adding a little adventure to their daily routine

- The city has over 40,000 outstanding warrants for people's arrest, largely for failing to pay traffic fines

- There are local Tucson citizens with non-violent backgrounds that are hindered from seeking new opportunities because of their criminal background

- People who have broken the law (former offenders) need a fresh start. Unfortunately, they often have outstanding fines that need to be paid to move to the next step

- Police officers and children need to build rapport, establish a community relationship, and reduce tension between teens and local police

- Local Christians need to network and collaborate with law enforcement, prosecutors, public defenders, probation officers, judges, pastors, and other partners of the criminal justice system to identify injustices and to create innovative strategies for reform

- A large percentage of the city's media and arts are not faith-based

- The story of God's blessings on the City of Tucson needs to be told through art and imagery

- Christians historically have failed to shape current perspectives of the City of Tucson because they have been reluctant to take part in the fields of media, literature, music, and arts

- Arts are influencers and often predictors of future cultural behavior; however, many times culture is not representative of Christian values

- A low percentage of Christian funding being utilized on city transformation

- Overall giving in Tucson is estimated at 2.8 percent

- Debt is crippling Christian individuals and families and keeps them from being generous to others

- Generosity allows people to feel a sense of hope, but without it, despair can create isolation within people

- Tucsonans need to know that when we pray God promises to respond; He is good, He loves us, and we can trust Him

- Tucsonans need to know that God has answers for all our city's challenges, in every domain, and He invites us to seek His counsel

- Tucsonans need to be able to see prayer as a gift God gives us

- Generation after generation of Tucsonans need to know about people who are local heroes of faith, people who have been used by God to bless Tucson, and encourage followers of Jesus to make a difference in their own generation

- Tucsonans must find tangible ways to foster the narrative of God's love for and pursuit of the people of Tucson

- A large number of residents are experiencing social isolation

- A large percentage of city residents are experiencing poverty

- A low percentage of Christian nonprofits are equipped to address city issues

- Neighborhoods are filled with children without things that can engage them in healthy outdoor activities

- Children need healthy adults to engage them in healthy activities

- Christian coaches (who lead by godly example) need support and encouragement

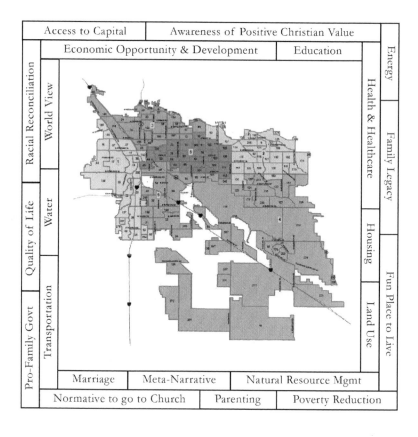

TUCSON'S CITY TRANSFORMATION STRATEGY

GOALS

- To address our city's most difficult and systemic problems (22-Focus Areas) by uniting Christians to envision and implement biblical solutions for the benefit of the entire city.

- Raise up 144,000 Partners.

- Develop a $15.8M Budget.

OUTPUTS

- *Domains:* a) Individual (Support)—"help" provided to just one member (person) or a larger group (organization) and b) Relational (Interaction)—the way in which two or more people or groups are influenced to talk to, behave toward, and deal with each other

- *Taskforces and Transformation Teams:* a) Structural (Design)—relates to the way something is built or organized: relating to the structure of something and b) Systemic (Outputs)—relates to an entire system's production (what it produces)

OUTCOMES

The rebuilding of these 22 focus areas of the city would restore Tucsonan's psychological, emotional, physical, and spiritual well-being concerning their relationship with God.

- Access to Capital
- City Awareness of Positive Christian Value
- Economic Opportunity and Development
- Education
- Energy
- Family Legacy
- Fun Place to Live
- Health and Healthcare
- Housing

- Land Use
- Marriage
- Meta-Narrative
- Natural Resource Management
- Normative to go to Church
- Parenting
- Poverty Reduction
- Pro-Family Government
- Quality of Life
- Racial Reconciliation
- Transportation
- Water
- World View

TUCSON'S CITY TRANSFORMATION METHODS

- *Awareness of City Issues/Challenges*—Examining sources of information.

- *Surveying and Analyzing the City's Issues/Challenges*—Researching city issues/challenges.

- *Seeking God*—How Christians should respond to city transformation issues/challenges.

- *Understanding the Complexities of an Environment (autonomy, authority, capacity, etc.)*—The importance of Christians being aware of their environment.

- *Repentance Before God*—Why it's important to humble yourself before God and ask for forgiveness before trying to solve city issues/challenges.

- *Restoration and Favor from God*—Why it's important to ask God for restoration and favor before trying to solve city issues/challenges.

- *Understanding and Submitting to God's Authority (and those with authority)*—Why it's important to submit yourself to God's authority before trying to solve city issues/challenges.

- *Inspiring People to Participate in Solving Issues/Challenges and Executing the Plan*—How to inspire people to participate in solving city issues/challenges.

- *Meeting with Tucson's City Leaders*—What it means to meet with city leaders.

- *Asking Those in Authority for Assistance*—Why it's important to ask those in authority for assistance in solving city issues/challenges.

- *Seeking God and Learning how to Respond to Opposition*—How to seek God when encountering opposition to solving city issues/challenges.

70201580R00125

Made in the USA
Columbia, SC
01 May 2017